THE JOY OF TEACHING

A Chorus of Voices

Edited by

John Cartafalsa
Lynne Anderson

University Press of America,® Inc.
Lanham · Boulder · New York · Toronto · Plymouth, UK

Copyright © 2007 by
University Press of America,® Inc.
4501 Forbes Boulevard
Suite 200
Lanham, Maryland 20706
UPA Acquisitions Department (301) 459-3366

Estover Road
Plymouth PL6 7PY
United Kingdom

Library of Congress Control Number: 2006933313
ISBN-13: 978-0-7618-3643-8 (paperback : alk. paper)
ISBN-10: 0-7618-3643-8 (paperback : alk. paper)

⊖™ The paper used in this publication meets the minimum
requirements of American National Standard for Information
Sciences—Permanence of Paper for Printed Library Materials,
ANSI Z39.48—1984

Contents

Foreword

W hat attracts teachers to their profession and keeps them coming back year after year? That is a key question that educators, school administrators and concerned parents are asking as the nation faces a critical teacher shortage.

To discover what draws teachers to the classroom, National University surveyed more than 15,000 alumni who had completed their teaching credentials in the past 30 years. Those who currently teach were asked to explain what keeps them faithful to their calling. Almost half of the respondents said that they remain on the job because they love working with children, or because of the personal reward and satisfaction they receive.

Today's teachers shoulder enormous responsibilities and bare unprecedented scrutiny. The future success of each student and, arguably, the future success of society itself are entrusted to them on a daily basis. There are numerous and often conflicting demands from students, parents and administrators which must be met and the pay is often less than teachers could make in other professions. It is encouraging to know that many teachers return to school every semester drawn by a passion for what they do.

Those who educate teachers are fortunate to share in their personal satisfaction and rewards. It is compelling when a biotech executive sacrifices two-thirds of her income to become a science teacher, then boasts that it was the best decision she ever made. It is worth repeating when a teacher describes the moment in which his student suddenly comprehended a complex lesson as "almost a religious experience." The elated expression on a student's face at that magical point of discovery, teachers say, is a tangible reward in its own right. That message needs to be amplified.

It has been reported that within this first decade of the new millennium more than two million new teachers must be hired to meet the coming demand. If schools are going to recruit and retain the most talented and inspiring individuals to fill these numerous positions, then the gratifying occasions and outcomes they will face must be captured and presented to a larger audience. I applaud the authors, for that is precisely their intention.

Jerry C. Lee, Ed.D.
Chancellor, National University System
President, National University

Prologue

BY JOHN CARTAFALSA

Ten years of continuing attendance and participation in presentations at the Lilly Conference, University of Miami, Oxford, Ohio, germinated the idea for "The Joy of Teaching: A Chorus of Voices." As co-editors, Lynne Anderson and I had heard presentations by teachers who had inspired us, some of whom were new to the Lilly Conference and others, like us, had returned and presented year after year. Magically, we experienced the impact the presenters had on us and others with repeated visits to their sessions! These presenters had changed our teaching and how we thought about teaching! We were moved to ask the question, "What will come of this activity?"

As one of our presenters said, "After you ask the question, you have the responsibility for finding answers." We did; we sought answers and arrived at a dialogue with each of the outstanding presenters . . . in our eyes and many others as we had observed. Was there a willingness to tell the tales of teaching from the perspective of a well-respected Lilly Conference presenter? Oh yes, indeed, there was willingness. From an immediate positive response to "Let me think about the idea," to "I'd like to, but I'm personally not in a position to do so at this time." Everyone we talked with liked the idea of telling his/her teaching story.

We were also inspired to action by the early passing of one of the greatest teachers among long-termed Lilly presenters, Beverly Firestone. She fought and lost a long battle with cancer. She presented with us until the very end. She gave courage to us as teachers and she taught us the life we gain from teaching. Beverly inspired us and we pulled the throttle out, full speed, on our creativity under her tutelage. We thank her as she provided inspiration to be diligent in our pursuit of this anthology.

We had to arrange for an editor and publisher for the collection of teaching stories. That was the easy part. What was difficult was staying in touch with the presenters and having each presenter get feedback and revise their stories according to editorial comments. Each presenter leads a multifaceted, highly thoughtful and productive life. Fitting in the telling of one's teaching story was not easy! And the reader will experience the reasons behind this difficulty. Each presenter shared deep thoughts about his/her journey through becoming so respected before their audiences. These stories took time, nearly three years from inception to publication, and a look deep into one's psyche and one's social behavior in order to understand the changes that one had made in becoming a truly wonderful, inspiring teacher. We had to leave behind some of the great among the group because their lives were just too complicated to complete their stories. Our hope is that they will be the first within the next book, "The Joy of Teaching II: A Chorus of Voices."

All presenters were able to share parts of their stories at special presentations at the Lilly Conference. We thought those stories were powerful and would impact others in their journeys to becoming truly wonderful, inspiring teachers. We believe that readers will enjoy and find meaning in the stories as each of them is different.

One story lingers and brings profound blessings to us; that is, the story by our featured author, Anthony Grasha. Our blessing is that we have his thoughts at his best. He asked us to accommodate his busy schedule by e-mailing questions to his conference site at Vancouver, WA, so he could meet our deadlines. He interrupted his conference activities five times with responses to each of our five probing questions in the revelation of his teaching story! As the e-mails were very promptly returned, we were moved to tears by the powerful, deeply rooted responses. His story is untouched as it is brought to you, the reader. We mourn his loss, as he died within the period of the book's developmental phases. His story and his teachings to us are what we cling to in gratitude for his gifts to our teachings.

We want to thank our incredible colleagues for their gifts to us as we share those gifts with you, the reader. Thank you for caring about teaching and teachers by reading the stories of some of the great among us.

Chapter 1

My Best Teacher, Ed Cushing

By Lynne Anderson

Of course, I have been impacted by a teacher who exemplified behavior I have chosen to emulate. He was Ed Cushing, a paleontologist at the University of Minnesota where I received my Master's degree and doctorate. In my first class with Ed, the chairs were arranged in a circle with his name, Ed, on an 8 ½ x 11 sheet of paper taped to his chair. He had no paper, no pencil, no tools of any kind. He was just there! His agenda was on his mind and in his heart. He smiled broadly as he began the class. Ed had a take home exam which I took seriously. When I picked up my final, he had a grade of "A" with the following comment: "This is a fine regurgitation of the book. However, I really wanted to hear from you."

Unforgettable!! He served on my doctoral committee and brought a refreshing dialogue with a question, "What is an apple?" At the close of my oral exam, my advisor said that was one of three best exams of its type for ten years! Ed initiated a wonderful conversation among academic people.

I begin class with a smile.
I use my first name with students.
I have students sit in circles.
I like to hear from students about what they think.
I like to add questions that evoke real dialogue.

* * * * *

Lynne Anderson serves as one of the editors for this anthology. Trained as a scientist at the University of Minnesota, her focus has been on teaching. Graduating from Moorhead, Minnesota, State University in science and mathematics education, her teaching career began at age twenty. Lynne has earned a doctorate in Educational Administration, also from the University of Minnesota. Her teaching and administrative experience spans nine private and public Minnesota and California high schools with an array of assignments. She has spent the past dozen years with National University teaching in the School of Education at the San Bernardino Center with the rank of Professor. Though honors have come her way, her greatest rewards have been sharing the success of the teachers and administrators she has helped train.

Chapter 2

Chaucer and the (He)art of Teaching: A Professor and Student in Dialogue

By Peter G. Beidler and Sierra Gitlin

This epistolary essay grows from *English 327: Chaucer*, a course taught by Professor Pete Beidler at Lehigh University in the fall of 2001, a course almost blown apart by the events of September 11. One of Pete's students that semester was a junior named Sierra Gitlin. At the time of the e-letters that make up this essay, Sierra was living in Nevada. The letters, all written between January 20 and February 12, 2002, have been shortened and somewhat revised for this published version. In her last letter on February 12, Sierra wrote, "My heart has been altered not for a couple of beats, but for good." To find out why she said that, read the correspondence that led up to it.

Dear Sierra:

I want to talk with you about our Chaucer class this past semester. Right after a course ends, while it is still fresh in my mind, I always try to reflect on what worked and didn't work. You recall that I distributed to you and your fellow students on the last day of class the standard machine-graded course evaluation forms. I just got them back. The evaluations were pleasantly positive, but there was so much the evaluation forms left out. In jotting some ideas down I found that something was missing—the student's voice. I could hum about the course from my side of my desk, but I want, rather, to be part of a duet. Would you like to be part of a series of e-letters about that course? Why you, of all the thirty five in that class? Well, mostly because you are honest and serious and I would very much value your opinions. But also because you are a good writer and are thinking of becoming a teacher. Are you interested in corresponding with me?

Sierra:

Absolutely. I would enjoy that. I really am hoping to be a teacher, and it would be good for me to chat with you about the Chaucer course. You brought out the best in me last semester. You made me strive to be the smartest person in the class, to write the best papers, to give the most insightful answers. I'm sure I did not succeed in those ambitions, but I do know that only a few teachers invoke my intellectual ruthlessness. You were one of them, and I'd like to reflect on how you did it.

Pete:

Let's get started, then. I don't recall that anyone has before accused me of inspiring "intellectual ruthlessness," but I think I know what you mean, and I think I am pleased.

My first impression of you was your unusual name "Sierra" on the course roster. I'd never known a Sierra before. Also, you sat tall and alert in the second row, to the left of center. I wonder if students realize how important it is to teachers to have students like you in a class, students who react and respond, whose faces speak even when their voices are quiet, who work their hearts out and never complain, who give their professors the benefit of the doubt, the chance to prove themselves

Sierra:

Did I do all that? I thought I was just sitting close to the door.

Pete:

Anyhow, you may remember that in that first class I gave you all a little questionnaire inviting each of you to tell me something special about yourselves, something you thought no one else could say. Your response, when I read it later that day back in my office, impressed me: "I am probably," you wrote, "the only student in this class who never graduated from high school." Yes, you got my attention with that one. I knew that I would have to find out something about your story before the end of the course.

Perhaps you would like to start by telling me your first impression of that course and of me.

Sierra:

My first impression came before the class started, before I met you. Your reputation preceded you, though only in the vague sense of "Beidler, yeah, everyone wants to take Chaucer." I thought, "He must be something special to inspire so many students voluntarily to take a class in which they're required to learn Middle English." And it was true, that windowless room was packed—to my dismay. Where were those small classes the school was always touting?

Anyhow, you made us all laugh that first day. You looked the part of the English professor to the letter. You were funny and irreverent. You put us at ease, and I knew I'd like you, even though the course material terrified me. "I will not be able to master Middle English," I fretted. Intimidated, I toyed with the idea of dropping the class. I wonder how many students Chaucer has sent crying to the registrar's office over the years.

Pete:

I am really glad you did not drop that course, Sierra. Three students did drop after that first class, and I never saw them again. I am always distressed when someone drops that course, for whatever reason. When that happens I feel like a failure as a teacher and a traitor to Chaucer, one of the finest writers who ever lived. He took twenty-nine pilgrims on a journey to Canterbury to pay homage at the cathedral shrine of St. Thomas. I have had the pleasure of taking two generations of students on a pilgrimage to the *Canterbury Tales*—a kind of literary shrine to Chaucer. I hate to see student-pilgrims drop by the wayside.

But you stayed put, and I am glad. If you hadn't, I would never have gotten to know you. I would never have heard you speak Middle English or found out why you never graduated from high school.

Lots of fine people do not graduate from high school, of course, but such folks rarely wind up at Lehigh, a pretty selective university. How had you gotten in? I wondered whether your daddy might be a wealthy and influential member of the Lehigh Board of Trustees or something, but I didn't remember any Gitlins on the Board.

Later I did learn just a little about your history. You said something about an unusual high school career and about dropping out. Do you want to tell me any of the details about how you got into Lehigh without graduating from high school?

Sierra:

You don't want to know all of the gory details. Let's just say my high school years were different from those of my Lehigh classmates. They weren't even spent in high school, for the most part. I attended two selective New England boarding schools and one regular public school before dropping out for good in November of my junior year. It is hard to say now whether my ailment was just a particular sensitivity to the usual tumult of adolescence or whether I suffered from the clinical depression I was diagnosed with, but for whatever reason I became utterly unable to function. A constant vacillation between intolerable sadness, happiness that bordered on mania, and anger beyond all reason were facts of my teenage life, as were the selfdestructive habits that so often accompany depression.

I had been on antidepressant drugs since my freshman year in high school, and the psychiatrist I was seeing at the time I dropped out was either particularly sadistic or completely incompetent. He gave me a crash course in SSRI's (in other words, a quick progression from one antidepressant to the next, without the proper weaning on and off). I became physically ill and mentally incapable of coping. Going to school was simply not a possibility. While my former classmates were trying on prom dresses and graduation robes, I was trying on adulthood in Boston, working, playing, and indulging in various self-destructive behaviors.

For four years, I worked at several jobs, spent the money I made on trips to Europe, and got a sense of a wider world.

Pete:

I am so happy that somehow you survived, Sierra. Sounds like you will someday need to write a book about those years.

Sierra:

I am not sure writing that book would be such a good idea, Pete. Some stories are perhaps better off forgotten. But my strange story has a happy ending. I eventually passed the GED test and enrolled in my local community college. I changed and grew, fell in love, and became happier than I ever thought I could be. I earned straight A's without too much effort and won a couple of awards for writing. I applied to "highly selective" Lehigh without any expectation that I would get in. Lehigh took a chance on me.

No, my father is about as far from being a wealthy and influential member of the Lehigh Board of Trustees as one could get, but he is a great cheerleader. He believed in me when I gave him every reason not to. And now I'm happy to say he has reason to once again.

Pete:

You are what the life of a teacher is all about. I wonder if I would have seen that glint in your eye that first day in our course if you *had* graduated from one of those expensive private prep schools. If I hadn't noticed something deeper in your eyes than in the eyes of others, would we be having this exchange of letters now?

When you become a teacher, you will understand your students better than if you had followed a happier trail in high school. When you write—and you will—you will have far more to say than someone who giggled her way through her teenage years.

But let's get back to Chaucer. Chaucer showed us that, despite the terrible difficulties people find themselves in, most stories have happy endings. I have always thought that great writers, like great teachers, help us learn how to live our lives. I am curious about whether, in the course of our course on Chaucer's *Canterbury Tales*, you picked up any pointers about how to live your life. Chaucer tells a lot of funny, raunchy, romantic, adventurous little stories, and sometimes one of them hits home. Did any of them hit Sierra? Did that dead white male who lived 600 years ago touch your heart?

Sierra:

That dead white male challenged me more than I had ever been academically challenged before. And I won. I know it wasn't a contest to see who could understand Chaucer best, who could write about Chaucer most brilliantly, or who could love Chaucer most. But on that first day of class, when changing my schedule seemed so much easier than learning Middle English only so I could read some arcane old tales in a language no one speaks any more, I began a contest with myself.

After a couple of class meetings, Middle English started to come easier. I began to notice the origins of many modern words, to see the connections between French and English and Latin. It was incredibly exciting for me. I have always loved words, loved the frequent absurdity of English, and learning to read Middle English was like watching the birth of my language.

To me, the strongest message that came through the tales themselves has to do with *authenticity*. I think the pilgrims and the characters in their tales embody different levels of genuineness, from the all-out deception of the lecherous monk in the *Shipman's Tale* to the delightful take-it-or-leave-it mentality of the Wife of Bath. In reading the tales, I found myself noting the differences in the authenticity of the characters and thinking a lot about my own authenticity.

I am different from the person I was a few years ago, so different I sometimes can't believe this life is really a continuation of that old life. Is the authentic Sierra this good person, this happy woman who loves English and learning and life, or is she that nihilistic and miserable teenager who was nearly destroyed by something that would eventually make her stronger? And if the answer is somewhere in between, that I am both, then do I hide the other parts, as the deceptive monk does, or announce them proudly and without regret, as the brazen Wife of Bath does?

In your entertaining (and to some prudish students, offensive) style, you pointed out the ways that Chaucer's characters are much like people today. They are faced with the same struggles: lust, morality, debt, death, flatulence, duty, and reconciling the differences between men and women. You make Chaucer seem surprisingly modern—sometimes even more modern than some "live" white males!

Pete:

Sierra, you just knock me down sometimes. It is amazing how little we teachers really know about what impression we make or whether our courses are "working" for our students. You have no idea how pleasing it is to hear you talk like that about Chaucer, his old language, his new ideas, his eternal characters, his modernity.

And as for *authenticity*, I don't remember using that word the whole semester long in that course, and you come along and pinpoint authenticity as what Chaucer was writing about. And of course you are right. Chaucer was concerned about authenticity in virtually all of his tales. Palamon was an authentic lover of Emily in the *Knight's Tale*, while Arcite was not. Nicholas, the horny college kid, was authentic in his lust for Alisoun in the *Miller's Tale*, while Absolon, the fruity parish clerk, was not. And so on. You just taught me something about a writer I have been studying for longer than you have been alive. And can you imagine how pleased I am to have someone of your generation tell me that one very special dead white male has a lot more on the ball than lots of living ones? Yep, you knock me down.

Sierra:
Good! Isn't language amazing? You just said that you'd been knocked down by a woman—and meant it as a compliment!

Pete:
I'd like to talk a bit more about that first day that nearly sent you to the registrar to drop Chaucer. I remember that many of my own teachers would just talk about how many papers were due, announce the attendance policy, hand out the syllabus, and say, "See you next time." I used to do that, but eventually came to see that I was losing a good opportunity to get a good start on the course. I spent our whole first class telling you about Middle English. I used strange terms like "the Great Vowel Shift," "phonetic transcription," the "International Phonetic Alphabet" and "French loan words." I wanted you to understand that we needed a phonetic alphabet because modern spelling is most definitely NOT a reliable guide to the way a word is pronounced. I suppose my behavior must have seemed calculated to get people to drop a course, but that was not my plan at all.

My plan was to help you understand, right from the start, the reading I had assigned for the second day, knowing that some people learn better by hearing something than they do just by reading. And, of course, I wanted to let you all know that this course was not like other English courses, since this one involved Middle English. But mostly I wanted to challenge you all, to let you know that if you tried, you could learn this new old language and read the great work of a great poet in the language he wrote it in, rather than in modern mistranslation. I wanted you to learn confidence by doing something that seemed really difficult, but that you could succeed at with a little effort. And I wanted you to know that any new subject makes us feel kind of dumb by humiliating us before it begins to make us feel smart by mastering it.

Did I make you feel dumb that first day of class?

Sierra:

More challenged than dumb. You had written a sentence on the board to introduce us to the phonetic alphabet: "A rough dough faced thoughtful ploughman strode through the town of Scarborough coughing and hiccoughing." I laughed out loud when I realized where you were going with that. It is eight different ways to pronounce the modern combination of letters "o-u-g-h." You were trying to show us why we needed a phonetic alphabet to indicate, as modern spelling cannot, what the sound of certain words was. I was intimidated and had already resigned myself to having my GPA lowered by your class. Ugh!—that's spelled "u-g-h." I wanted to know more about the Great Vowel Shift. I wanted to prove to you and to myself that I could learn to read Middle English. To be honest, however, I'm surprised you lost only three people after that first day.

But I have a question for you. How do you stand up there and tell a room of thirty-odd college students that before they can even start on the actual "Chaucer" part of the Chaucer course, they have to learn this phonetic alphabet, use it to transcribe Middle English sounds, and be tested on it? Your detailed syllabus said that the assignment for our second class would require that students take several hours working through the various rules for pronouncing and transcribing Chaucer's Middle English and then apply them to the words in the exercise due the next class. I would have been scared of losing all of the students!

Pete:

I was scared. But I really do feel that students of Chaucer should learn how to pronounce Chaucerian Middle English and that the best way for me to help them do that is to use the International Phonetic Alphabet, where each letter or symbol represents only one sound.

Sierra:

Anyhow, don't you ever envy the professors who teach classes that seem more attuned to the mentality of the average college student? Wouldn't it be easier to stand at the front of the classroom and say "Welcome to *Gender in the American Horror Film*? This semester, we'll be watching lots of scary movies as a way to understand gender relationships." YOU know, and now I know, that Chaucer is perfectly attuned to the college student's mentality, once you get by the fact that it takes lots of work even to start to understand what he was saying. But don't you get scared, standing up there and talking about phonetic alphabets and daily quizzes and memorizing the list of 130 common Middle English words? Aren't you afraid we'll shoot the messenger before we hear the postscript to the message: that all the hard work will pay off in confidence and fun and knowledge?

I stayed because I wanted to earn bragging rights as one of the very few people in the world who could read Middle English. But why in the world did those others stay on? And you, how do you go through with it year after year? What is it that spurs you on to create willing minds out of ones that, on day one, are so stubbornly closed?

Pete:

You just answered your own question, didn't you? I love the chance to create willing minds out of ones that are so stubbornly closed.

Do I sometimes wish I were teaching a subject matter that would automatically be more appealing to modern students? Well, of course, I do teach such courses. My course in contemporary Native American fiction has a sticker appeal that Chaucer can never have. But I know that I am doing the right thing by teaching Chaucer.

For one thing, I know that Chaucer will still be with us, still be read and taught, long after some of the modern stuff has faded into obscurity. For another, I feel really NEEDED when I teach Chaucer. Chaucer NEEDS me more than, say, Hemingway needs me when I teach him because the language Chaucer wrote in now looks outdated, and because he was writing at the dawn of the British cultural and literary tradition. I have a job to do when I spread the delights of Chaucer before students who, without my help, see so little to delight in. I KNOW I can make modern students love medieval stories. I am like the little teaching engine that could. It is uphill at first, but I think I can, I think I can, I think I can. And then I KNOW I can, I KNOW I can, I KNOW I can.

I am trying to sound confident, Sierra, but as you have probably figured out, I am really a rat's nest of pedagogical insecurities. I never know if I am a good teacher, I never feel really comfortable in front of a class, and I sometimes wonder whether Chaucer is really relevant to the modern world. Why should I spend my thirty most productive years teaching Chaucer when I could be helping my fellow humans in some more direct way?

I felt that way particularly on September 11, a day that none of us will ever forget. Is it OK if we talk about that for a bit?

Sierra:

Absolutely. That class met twice a week, and September 11 was only our fifth meeting. I remember that class with a slow-motion clarity that is often the product of such scary circumstances, but, unfortunately, your lecture isn't part of my recollection.

Pete:

I don't remember much of what I talked about, either. An hour before I walked down the hill to our Chaucer class, I heard that the World Trade Center had been hit, though at that point no one really knew if it was a bomb or an accident. A half hour before I walked down the hill to our Chaucer class, I heard from my wife that our son Kurt was "in Manhattan, in that vicinity." Surely you noticed that I was acting pretty weird that day. We were supposed to be talking about the language in Chaucer's *Knight's Tale* or something stupid like that, and here America and my own family seemed to be under attack.

The *Knight's Tale* is about love and fighting, but that day in class I was feeling more fear than love; I was concerned about what sort of battle was going on in New York rather than the one in ancient Greece. At the start of the *Knight's Tale*, the evil Creon will not let the Theban widows bury the dead bodies of their slain sons and husbands, but who was the evil Creon in New York who had already buried untold thousands of men and women in a heap of dusty rubble? These were not literary deaths we were dealing with, but real ones, probably involving people some of us in the class knew. I was feeling useless and helpless and full of fear.

During that class I did not know what I was doing. Teaching Chaucer was the very last thing I felt like doing, yet as a teacher of Chaucer it seemed that teaching Chaucer was what I *should* be doing.

I told you students what was going on in New York, though most of you already knew, and I mentioned that my son was in there someplace. I told you that you could leave if you needed to and then charged ahead with the *Knight's Tale*. But my heart was not in it. I got through that seventy-five minutes somehow, but for the next several weeks, I felt that I had chosen the wrong profession. I could not think of a single reason to go on teaching Chaucer in a world suddenly come apart, suddenly collapsed into bloody rubble.

Sierra:

During that class I couldn't think of anything but my absolute need to get to a radio or TV to find out what was going on. I do remember when you told us that your son was in Manhattan. You almost broke down. I felt this urge to put my arm around you and say, "It's OK, Pete. We don't have to do this today. Go home and be with your family."

I felt badly for you, and couldn't understand how you could possibly switch off the panic and talk about Chaucer. It seemed like you felt obligated to go on with class for our sake, and I just wanted someone to tell you that you didn't have to. But I thought maybe you needed to do it and that maybe distracting yourself from the worry would be good for you, and maybe good for us too.

Pete:

I don't know if it helped me or not to go on. I don't know if it helped you.

Sierra:

At the time, I wished you would stop talking about Chaucer and let us go. I was fighting back tears and the urge to run out and find a CNN station. As for the weeks following that day, like you, I couldn't think of a single reason to go on learning Chaucer. Or anything else. In the face of such horror and sadness and uncertainty, nothing really seemed worth doing.

But just as Chaucer and my other classes seemed in some ways irrelevant, I was able to derive some perspective and comfort from them. For instance, when I read Chaucer's words, which had survived 600 years, I somehow felt a sense of both the permanent and the ephemeral. Who would have thought something as "permanent" as the Twin Towers could be lost in a moment? Who would have thought that the bits of calfskin that Chaucer's works were written on could survive so long?

Anyhow, thinking about Chaucer, I felt a sense of belonging, not just to the time in which I live, but to a very long procession of lives—an endless succession of tragedy and joy and hope and death and rebirth. For these reasons, I was able to continue studying Chaucer in a world where, yes, almost everything felt suddenly irrelevant. Chaucer couldn't have thought his stories would be the topic of college courses 600 years after his death. That reminded me that the things we do matter in ways we cannot predict. Perhaps, I thought, the times when our lives seem most irrelevant are the times when our actions matter most. So, I guess what I'm saying is I'm glad we went on with the Chaucer class. Perhaps it was the only choice we could have made.

Pete:

I leave most classes feeling vaguely depressed. I replay the class in my mind, thinking of the things I might have said but didn't, or I imagine that something I did say may have offended someone, or I wonder how I could have gotten a certain point over more clearly or why I can't seem to get more than the same old one-third of the class to say anything.

I felt particularly troubled about my performance that day. My mind was one-third on Chaucer, one-third on the safety of my son, and one-third on the larger horror in Manhattan. I did not learn of the attack on the Pentagon or the crash in western Pennsylvania until after I left class, so those had no share of my thinking yet.

It may be that if you don't remember a single thing I said in class about Chaucer, it is because I didn't really say anything at all. I vaguely recall that I did end the class early. I suppose I could have just cancelled the whole thing, but I have deeply ingrained in my sense of my profession the notion that teachers teach. That is just what we do, and I could not think of any reason to take a vacation that day. That shows how twisted my logic was, doesn't it? I had a ton of reasons to give us all a "vacation" that day, but I didn't. I couldn't.

Sierra:

Don't be so hard on yourself, Pete. You did fine and we all appreciate your dedication to your profession, even if we did not quite understand it at that time in that context. But your concern suggests something I'd like to ask you about. Sometimes you seem really insecure about your teaching. You're clearly one of the best professors anywhere. You are smart and passionate about what you do and about your students, but you sometimes seem uncertain. Is it that anything less than perfection feels like less than your best? Perhaps your insecurity means that you really care, but it puzzles me.

Pete:

I have never been confident about my teaching, and it still scares me to walk into a classroom. Yes, I guess I am a perfectionist about what I do. I shouldn't be, because I know that teaching is by nature a messy activity, one that depends on all sorts of factors outside of my control: the time of day, the physical setup of the classroom, the subject matter, the motivation of the students, the phase of the moon, and weird stuff like September 11. Still, there is much that I DO control, and it is good to get feedback about my teaching from students, the only people who really matter.

But I want to challenge you in a different direction now. Of course I like it when you say nice things about my teaching, but I have a different assignment as we come close to the end of our exchange. I want you to say something negative about me or the course.

That may be difficult for you. You and I are having this exchange because we like and admire each other. That is part of what the teaching is all about—that special bond that sometimes develops between teachers and students. You and I have that bond. You and I seemed to connect in really nice ways that semester. I like saying good things about you, and the feeling seems to be mutual. But it is important that you be critical of me and our course together. You want to be a teacher yourself. I know you will be a fine, fine teacher, but you will have to get tough with yourself from time to time. Practice by getting tough with me now.

So what did I do wrong? What were the weaknesses of the course or my approach to it? When you get to teach, what I did will you for sure NOT do, because you saw that it did not work or had bad effects which I did not know about?

Sierra:

Believe me, I would love to say something bad about you or your class, but honestly, I've been thinking since I got your letter, and all I can think of is that you might change the order in which you taught some of Chaucer's tales. I could come up with only one thing of any importance. I am not sure if it is a criticism. I guess it is just a question I'd like you to answer.

You remember in an earlier letter you asked me whether Chaucer had touched my heart? That question puzzled me, and I avoided it then. I like it that you try to connect to the emotional sides of your students, to their hearts. But what about our minds? Am I wrong to sense that you are somehow less interested in my growing intellectually than in my growing emotionally?

Pete:

My goodness, you *are* perceptive, aren't you, Sierra? You and I may be destined to differ on this matter. What was the term you used back in one of your early letters?—that I had brought out your "intellectual ruthlessness." You meant it as a compliment, and I took it as such, but we do seem to be thinking of teaching in two somewhat different registers. I AM interested in your mind, of course. I suppose it is the minds of my students that I should be centrally interested in. I want to give, or lead you to, the obvious stuff: a sense of the origins of English literature and the joys of poetry. I want to help you sharpen your critical reading and thinking and writing skills, and so on. That intellectual stuff is important, of course, and it is what I grade you on. But I really find, as I grow older, that it is the hearts of my students that I am most interested in. I don't know that I can remember much at all about any specific thing any of my own teachers taught me, but I remember the ones who cared—about their subject, about their teaching, and especially about me.

Having this epistolary conversation with you has helped me to realize something. It has helped me to see that, while Chaucer is great, you and my other students are greater. I care less about Chaucer's language than about yours, less about him than about you. His time is past. Yours is now. It is you and your future and your sense of values and your ability to change the hearts of others that I care most about.

Sierra:

I guess I knew that, and I respect that. But how do you grade our hearts?

Pete:

I don't, of course. And I know that something is wrong with this picture. I grade your mind, your intellectual performance, but I care about your heart, your emotional growth.

Is there any reason I should not admit that I am less interested in teaching your mind than in teaching your heart? You have a wonderful mind. I suppose I had a few things to offer it last semester.

But you also brought a sensitive heart to my Chaucer course. I'd *like* to think that I may have helped your heart to feel something new, a love for Chaucer, yes. A love for some fellow humans who lived six centuries ago, of course. A love for some twentieth-century fellow pilgrims that you may not have felt before, absolutely.

I'd like to have altered your heart, and the hearts of a few of your classmates, just for a couple of beats, Sierra.

Sierra:
Well, you did. My heart has been altered not for just a couple of beats, but for good.

* * * * *

Pete Beidler has been teaching at Lehigh since the late 1960s. He specializes in Chaucer studies and contemporary Native American literature. In 1983, he was named National Professor of the Year by the Carnegie Foundation and CASE (Council for the Advancement and Support of Education). He taught at Sichuan University in Chengdu, China, as a Fulbright professor in 1987-88, and at Baylor University in 1995-96 as the Robert Foster Cherry Visiting Distinguished Professor. Since 1978, he has held the Lucy G. Moses Chair at Lehigh.

Sierra Gitlin majored in English at Lehigh before moving to the Lake Tahoe area of Nevada, where she has just completed her undergraduate degree at the University of Nevada, Reno. She is an avid skier and mountain biker and also does freelance writing. She and Gregg enjoy running after their rambunctious golden retriever, Maceo.

Chapter 3

Reflections on "A Last Lecture" and an Odyssey through Academe

By Linc Fisch

I've occasionally posed this question to a faculty colleague: "If you were to prepare your very last lecture for your students, what would be the three or four main concepts or components of it—i.e., what are the most important things you want them to have learned in your courses?" Such a reflective exercise is useful because, in clarifying one's most important goals, it helps to ensure that these components will be appropriately emphasized in-course, as well as reinforced in a capstone session at the end.

(As an aside, I find it unusual and revealing that most of us seldom use our final class moments to cap a course with crème de la crème material and send students off on a high note. Instead, we usually close with exam-preparation tips or with the examination itself, both of which are likely fraught with student anxiety. But, I digress.)

Having suggested the last-lecture exercise to some of my colleagues, it seemed sensible that I also turn the question onto myself. As I've often learned from trying to answer questions that I've framed for others, the question may not be stated carefully enough to draw a valid response. In this instance in particular, many faculty members do not "lecture" in the traditional sense. I myself have often said, with tongue only partly in cheek, "I gave a lecture once, about forty years ago, and I swore that I'd never give another one." In truth, many college teachers find a mix of discussions, seminars, case studies, laboratories, projects, field experiences, independent study, and other active learning methods—sometimes strategically interspersed with lectures or mini-lectures—to be instructional modes of choice. Therefore, let me modify my question: If you were designing your very last meeting with your students, what would be the three or four main concepts or components of it?"

In my own response to this question, the concepts listed below are what I hope will stand out in students' minds as they leave my courses, and I hope these concepts will inform their future lives.

- Strive to fulfill the unique potential that is within you by discovering your personal strengths, talents, skills, and then employing them to the maximum extent possible. Try to find some activity to which your can devote yourself deeply and passionately. Constantly focus on improvement. Aim for excellence in all that you do.
- Resolve problems and make sound decisions based on respect for evidence and principles of critical reasoning. Encourage such reasoning in all groups of which you are a part. Be willing to consider and appropriately modify your decisions and actions in the light of changing circumstances. Evaluate not only the costs and benefits, but also possible consequences before undertaking risks.
- Act ethically, taking into account that almost all activities have subtle ethical dimensions. Recognize the values you hold, how they are in accord or in conflict with each other, and how they form your behavior. Weigh ethical situations carefully and thoroughly, and then make your best moral judgments.
- Serve others and society in any useful way you can. Share your knowledge, talents, skills, and resources with others. Make your brief stay on this planet count for something that will persist long after your physical person has departed.
- Continue throughout your life to learn and grow and develop, particularly from your experiences.

Oddly enough, only one or two of these might be linked in some way to specific contents of most of the mathematics courses I've taught. Few students (not even those in Father Guido Sarduccci's whimsical "Five-

Minute University") are likely to have need for the quadratic formula. Many calculus processes are instrumental only as means to more advanced concepts in mathematics and physics. On the other hand, many students will have the opportunity for application of problem solving strategies and for ethical uses of knowledge in everyday life.

Others who have engaged in a last-lecture exercise often have given responses similar to mine. The things that are really important, the things that we most hope students have acquired, are often not content matters, as such. They likely do not appear anywhere at all; they appear in a general catalog description of the goals of higher education, particularly a liberal arts education. Frequently, they are honored in first-year orientation speeches and in commencement addresses, but all too rarely are they explicitly dealt with in the classroom or in other contacts between students and faculty.

Of course, it would be difficult to address such goals adequately in a final class session, even if it were an extended seminar or workshop. Further, it would not be appropriate to deal with such matters only in a perfunctory way in a single session. These are goals that infuse all our classroom efforts, goals that are not attained through the normal strategies of lecture presentation. A final session, at most, may bring the concepts that underlie our teaching efforts throughout a term into a final, sharp, summary focus.

These are concepts that come to the fore in our discussions of issues and cases. They come to the fore in considering the practical applications of course content. They come to the fore when students begin to relate material to their own frames of reference. And perhaps most of all, they come to the fore in the person of the teacher, for as many of my colleagues attest, we really teach ourselves by how we design and conduct our courses, by the examples and models we present, and by the personal values that students read from our behavior.

The centrality of the student-teacher relationship in all matters of learning was well articulated in 1871 by James A. Garfield at a Williams College alumni meeting honoring their college president: " I am not willing that this discussion should be closed without mention of the value of a true teacher. Give me a log hut, with only a simple bench, Mark Hopkins on one end and I on the other, and you may have all the buildings, apparatus, and libraries without him." It has informed college teaching for well over a century.

Some teachers—fortunately only a few—inappropriately use the classroom to advocate their own values or otherwise attempt to indoctrinate students. Some will argue that the classroom should be completely free from the values of the teacher. Others will say that since it's practically impossible to do that, we should consciously filter or selectively choose the values we reveal to students. And still others insist that an important component of our teaching missions is to encourage and help our students to reflect on values, to decide for themselves and clarify their own values, to acknowledge these values and to commit firmly to them, and to learn how to apply them to practical situations. Eventually, I came to endorse this fourth viewpoint.

Engaging in a last-lecture exercise and reflecting thereon led me to explore how I came to college teaching as a career and why I continued in it in some form even beyond my retirement. My simple answer is likely little different from what my colleagues might say: expectation, encouragement, environment, and reinforcement.

My mother had only eighth-grade education in the small northern Ohio town where I was born. My father completed only four years of school in his Transylvanian village before his parents died and he came to America to carve out a new life, adding to his knowledge in various non-traditional ways. They both held high standards for me, including getting as much education as possible. And they held teaching in high regard.

The Carnegie Library in our town was relatively new during my childhood, and it was only a block and a half away from my house; I began walking there by myself and checking out books even before I started school. I could today walk unerringly to the building and into the room that held the children's books (and recently did just that, despite the library's having been expanding by a factor of at least five since I first visited it). When my family moved to a larger town, I quickly discovered that there was a branch library across the street from my junior high school, and I continued my frequent library visits. I distinctly recall staring longingly at the thickness of *Moby Dick* for months before finally taking the plunge and reading it, albeit with an eighth-grader's approach and frame of reference.

Because I seemed to exhibit a propensity for learning, my teachers at all educational levels, as well as other who knew me, encouraged me to embrace learning. Whenever I engaged in any teaching kind of activity I received feedback that was satisfying. Clearly I enjoyed learning, and I began to enjoy teaching. And that enjoyment was rooted quite early in my life, well before college and university.

The first "teaching" I can recall doing was during my first week of fourth grade. As I was walking home from school with a neighbor third-grader, I found myself explaining and discussing ideas about simple geography that he would soon be encountering. In Boy Scouts, I found myself helping other members master the skills and knowledge to advance in rank. Knowledge of plants joyously acquired on a chance field trip with a biology teacher helped me land a position as a camp counselor for two summers, where I became the resident botanist. Later, when I was in boot camp at a naval training station, my company commanders put me in charge of teaching knot tying and of drilling the company—skills that I had mastered in the Scouts and ROTC.

At the time, I don't think that I recognized that these events clearly pointed towards teaching as a possible career. Neither did I realize that there was something else lying below the surface as I pondered and explored what my goal or mission in life might be. At that time, I came up with only a rather simplistic "to do good."

I drifted through my college days without a precisely sharpened career goal in mind, taking courses I enjoyed, as many students do today. That's not necessarily a bad thing, of course, since college is a good time to explore many possibilities. When it came time to find a job, my experience as a teaching fellow and a house fellow in university led me to seriously consider and obtain a college teaching position. It just seemed to be the natural thing for me to do. (I hasten to add that teaching is not suitable for everyone. As A.A. Milne's astute but gloomy philosopher Eeyore observed, "We can't all, and some of us don't. That's all there is to it.")

As I grew older, my broader and deeper experiences translated into broader and deeper learning. I steadily expanded and refined "to do good" into a personal manifesto that incorporated the five clusters of concepts I've listed above. Although I didn't neglect my focus on science and technology, I became more and more interested in the process of learning and teaching—and particularly the human dimensions of those activities. And I realize that teaching was not only a means to disseminate and advance knowledge, but a way to amplify many times over one's own influence and contributions through the work of others—and thus achieve a sort of immortality, if you will.

However, my own journey through academe was far from linear. Instead of settling into teaching at a particular institution after a few years, I found myself periodically presented with new and interesting opportunities that took me in unanticipated directions and venues, including several years as an associate dean of students. A major turning point came in the mid-sixties when I was invited to teach a graduate seminar in dental education, supposedly a temporary assignment but one that lasted for over six years. My focus turned away from administration and back to teaching. I became involved in developing short, high impact, open-ended films to trigger discussion, which in turn led me into using the then-burgeoning television technology. Another spin-off was I discovered that I wrote best when I wrote succinctly and edited mercilessly. My learning to operate video cameras and managing discussions based on triggering stimuli resulted in my appointment to a position in a school of public health, where I helped design and teach the core curriculum, and I established and supervised an expanded audio-visual department in a recently opened new building. I had little training or preparation for most of these assignments, requiring me to quickly extrapolate from my experience in order to meet new challenges. Needless to say, it all became a glorious series of new learning events for me, each change bringing new satisfactions and generating new vigor. (It also was evident to bolster noted American philosopher Lawrence Peter Barra's famous injunction, "When you come to a fork in the road, take it.")

Years later, I found myself coming full circle: Eventually there came a time to leave professional education, and I returned to an early love, teaching undergraduate mathematics. And after several years of revalidating myself in this area and at this level, I moved on to working independently. (I frequently identified myself as "no longer institutionalized" even though a few of my dear friends often opine, "But maybe you should be.") I focused on conducting workshops for college faculty members, developing trigger films (and later case studies), and engaging in educational writing. Thus at retirement age and beyond, I found myself doing what I considered to be some of my best work, all of it growing out of diverse experience and most of it embodying the enduring concepts and values I had come to hold dear.

Can I extract meaning from all of this? Can I leave readers of this essay with last words that will remain with them and move them ever forward in their own academic journeys? Let me try.

- Discovering what things one can do well, particularly those that will benefit others, and then doing them, represents a great fulfillment of one's life. As a catchy phrase has it: A mind is a terrible thing to waste. Wasting skills and talents is also a terrible loss of resources.
- Experience is a wonderful teacher if we deliberately condition ourselves to learn from it. Habitual reflection and drawing meaning are the keys to learning.
- New challenges that are within one's range of capabilities stretch imagination and enhance perspective. Such opportunities often come from beyond one's own field of expertise. Being fully prepared for new challenges is not necessarily a prerequisite to accepting them; much growth comes from expanding one's knowledge and abilities in order to rise to the task. This requires openness, willingness, and even a bit of courage to take reasonable risks.
- The career of teaching offers many opportunities for affecting the future though the eventual work of our students. It represents a kind of power and empowering that, when used wisely, can transform lives.
- Teaching may not result in prominence, celebrity, wealth, or power in the usual sense. But it more than compensates through the satisfaction, sense of accomplishment, and intrinsic rewards that accrue from helping others grow and develop.
- In order to teach well or do anything well, for that matter, one has to love the activity and be fully committed to it. Teaching cannot be a routine or rote process, performed perfunctorily. It is a dynamic activity that requires constant adjustment, adaptation, and innovation.
- In the simplest way I can, I leave these imperatives: Learn, Live, Love, Grow, Create, Enjoy, and Share. And if you would be a part of one of the most noble and joyful enterprises in the world: Teach and Teach Well.

In retrospect, I realize that the people I remember and honor the most during my life have been my teachers or people who often functioned as teachers—parents, ministers, scoutmasters, YMCA officials, and yes, at times students and colleagues. We sat together on that simple bench, each of them in turn at one end and I on the other. They remain with me today as unseen presences, still guiding my life. Let us hope that our students will view us in the same way. If they do, we will have been successful in fulfilling our responsibilities to society.

Endnote

I have drawn from the wisdom of many others throughout my life. I share below the thoughts of a few who have figured prominently with regard to my reflections offered in this essay.

Not perfection as a final goal, but the ever enduring act of perfecting, maturing, refining is the aim of living.

> —John Dewey

Live as if you were to die tomorrow. Learn as if you were to live forever.

> —Mahandras Gandhi

There's a way to do it better. Find it.

> —Thomas Edison

A great discovery solves a problem, but there is a grain of discovery in the solution of any problem.

> —George Polya

For things we have to learn before we can do them, we learn by doing them.

> —Aristotle

Within the limits set by our innate abilities, we should strive for excellence, for the best we can do. Not for perfection—for that is almost always unattainable, and setting it as an aim can only lead to the distress of frustration. Excellence is a wonderful goal in itself and highly suitable to earn us the goodwill, respect, and even love of our neighbors.

> —Hans Selye

Chance favors only the mind which is prepared.

> —Louis Pastuer

I have found that though the ways in which I can make myself useful are few, yet the work open to me is endless. . . I long to accomplish a great and noble task, but it is my chief duty in life to accomplish humble tasks as though they were great and noble. The world is moved along not only by the mighty shoves of its heroes, but also by the aggregate of the tiny pushes of each honest worker.

—Helen Keller

Teaching really is a noble profession. It's a chance to enrich students' lives, an opportunity to affect eternity.

—Alfred Mitty

I have the power to nudge, to fan sparks, to praise an attempted answer, to condemn hiding from the truth, to suggest books, to point out a pathway. What other power matters?

—Peter Beider

A moral principle . . . is not a command to act or forbear acting in a given way; it is a tool for analyzing a special situation, the right or wrong determined by its entirety, not by the rule as such.

—John Dewey

We should so live and labor in our time
that what comes to us as seed may go to the next generation as blossom,
and what comes to us as blossom may go to them as fruit.

—Adapted from the poem
"I Will Not Die an Unlived Life"
by Dawna Markova
(paraphraser unknown)

* * * * *

Linc Fisch has retired from 40 years of teaching, program development, and administrative assignments in Ohio, Michigan, and Kentucky, but he continues to contribute to higher education through writing, conducting workshops for faculty, and designing films and interactive cases to trigger discussion. *The Chalk Dust Collection* (1996) is an accumulation of 35 of his short educational articles and columns. He edited and contributed to *Ethical Dimensions of College and University*

Teaching (1996). His column appears on a regular basis in the National *Teaching and Learning Forum* and *the Journal of Staff, Program, and Organization Development*. Fisch has a particular interest in issues dealing with ethics and values in college teaching.

Chapter 4

Untitled

By Tony Grasha*

Let me begin with my off-campus activities. Almost without exception, all conferences and workshops as well as campus visit sessions are evaluated. Those evaluations ask for information about the presenter, the content presented, facilities for the session, and a number of other issues. Responses of participants have been uniformly positive but there are also things people say that make me pause, think about what was said, and inevitably I make changes.

On the positive side, my presentation style is appreciated because I'm organized, enthusiastic about what I present, I have a good sense of humor, I use a lot of active learning strategies and most importantly—I never tell people what to do in their teaching. That is, while I have a lot of ideas about the teaching-learning process, I'm smart enough to know that ideas for teaching have to be filtered by the end-user. Teaching is not like following a recipe. Each "cook" has to bring his or her style to the task including adding new ingredients and at times messing with those in the recipe.

Thus, all of my sessions use reflective activities where people are asked to consider possible implications for their own teaching of the materials. Typically those activities involve moments of private reflec-

---

* Mr. Grasha passed away before completing the editing process for this chapter. The material is intact as he presented it to the editor.

tion followed by discussions in pairs or small groups with colleagues. In the latter case, they consult with each other on ideas for teaching implicit information presented. My role is then to answer questions and to clarify points about the content after such discussions take place.

I avoid answering questions such as, "How can I improve what I do by using your materials?" Or, "What's the best thing you do that I could use in my classroom?" All that trying to answer such questions does is open the conversation up to "Yes, but I tried that once and it did not work or I teach in a discipline outside of the social sciences and its much harder for me to teach in the ways you suggest." Rarely, either because of fatigue, or a lapse in judgment, when I took the bait and tried to make "helpful" suggestions, I typically regretted it.

What works best for me is to ask, "Tell me how you think you could use the information and what problems you might experience in doing so?" That opens the discussion for me to comment but also for others in the session to share their expertise. It seems to work since over the years people have remarked that they liked the way I created options but did not come across as having all of the answers.

The second thing I receive comments about is that I presented interesting information and allowed people to think about it and to work by themselves and with others on how to use it. Both are mentioned and in the context of "you practiced what you preached." That is, I allowed their independent, collaborative, and participatory learning styles to emerge in the session. And I reinforced and acknowledged those forms of learning as important.

I think there is a deeper reason for the latter comments. Teaching is a relatively lonely but public experience. That is, we teach with others present and we work with others who teach. Rarely do we really have a chance to sit down with colleagues and deconstruct our teaching processes. Most conversations about teaching outside of workshops and seminars are about specific techniques that either worked or did not work well or general observations about the process. Looking behind what is done for core principles and ideas is the exception rather than the rule. Also, doing so with one's colleagues in a supportive environment does not happen with a high degree of frequency. Most people are pretty much on their own and thus workshops and conference sessions where they can get "beneath the surface" are valuable. And, I think, really critical for anyone who wants to make dramatic changes in what they do in the classroom.

On the negative side, anywhere from 5-15 percent of those in attendance were not satisfied to varying degrees. Sometimes the things others liked were seen as negatives (e.g., independent thinking, working with colleagues) and at other times they did not see the relevance of the material for their teaching. In such cases, I either presented things they already know, did not provide enough depth for them, or they could not see its applications to their disciplines.

In my teaching of psychology subjects, I use a lot of active learning strategies and try to accommodate a variety of learning styles. For me keeping students actively engaged through small group projects and discussions, case studies, role playing, and other devices allows for a range of learning styles to get reinforced and for task engagement to occur. Quality time on tasks is still one of the best predictors of student achievement. And, using variety in how this is done accommodates a variety of learning styles and contributes to student motivation and satisfaction with learning.

Students appreciate the approach and it is one of the reasons my courses are over subscribed and why I've received a number of awards for teaching. Along with comments such as "I liked getting involved in class," "the term went so fast for me." "I could not just sit and take notes in your course, I had to be involved," "this is the best course I've taken" suggest that students appreciated the experiences I've provided.

The downside is that again 5-15 percent of those taking the courses to varying degrees did not like the approach. And, just like conference and workshop participants, they did so for the same reasons others liked it. My sense is that some students just wanted to be left alone, to take notes, and to come to class when they felt like it. In my learning style model, they are labeled avoidant learners but much more is going on there than a lack of interest. Some are overwhelmed with requirements in other courses or their jobs and are looking for breathing room in their schedules only to find I don't provide it. "The course took too much time," is a common comment. Others are anxious about performing in a course that has high demands for participation while a few want a standard college classroom experience.

I guess you can't please all of the people all of the time. But you can learn from your critics. In class and in workshops I avoid the trap of making 5-15 percent of the comments seem like a majority opinion. I do listen and I try to integrate lessons learned into the next round. In classes and workshops I make sure there are "mini-lectures" for those who want some didactic information or want to have my expertise in the fore-ground. I always ask groups to tell me about the advantages AND disadvantages of the using the information in their lives or their teaching. Whenever possible, I indicate there are options and alternative points of view on issues. This seems to help.

With colleagues at the University of Cincinnati, it has been a mixed bag. When I had institutional roles of running faculty development programs, those attending what my faulty development organization did were largely positive about the efforts. Those outside the loop were often critical believing that the money could be better spent on department initiatives rather than campus-wide activities. For them faculty development was a personal experience and could not be facilitated by others. Attendance at discipline conferences, academic leaves, funds for visiting speakers on discipline issues or an occasional teaching presentation were all that was needed. The value of an in-depth examination of teaching issues was not valued nor did it fit into the reward structure of the institution, as they understood it.

Within my department, I think that my teaching-learning activities at the local, regional, national and international level are known to people. But, there has never been a lot of active support or encouragement for the effort. One reason is that our department is not located in a college of education and thus the professional activities center around the discipline of psychology. Thus, my teaching-learning interests do not easily fit into the core of the undergraduate or graduate programs. That is, courses and programs dealing with such things are not a core part of the department's offerings. Human factors, neuropsychology, clinical psychology and other more traditional areas of the field dominate. Fortunately, I have expertise in cognitive and social psychology and conduct research and write in the latter areas as well. But the "teaching side of me" is just not core content.

In addition, teaching is pretty much perceived among my colleagues as a set of mechanical processes or methods used to present content. An exploration of the historical, philosophical, or theoretical issues behind the methods is not highly valued. This is largely due to the structure of the curriculum and little in the training or experiences of people to make this a high priority. Of course, the latter things are what interest me most and the mechanical techniques least. Thus, some perceptions are that what I do is understandably probably okay for others but not for them. There is a mismatch that is hard to overcome.

There are positive and negative memories at the department level. On the positive side has been recognition by students for a variety of teaching and mentoring awards the department gives. Several colleagues and I over the years have had wonderful interactions and discussions about teaching. Some have even tried some of the things I've suggested and I've learned from others ways to improve what I do. Those interactions have been delightful and engaging and fun.

On a less positive note, there is currently no formal training program for our graduate students in teaching. Over the years, I've offered a "hands-on" seminar on teaching processes but only a handful of graduate students from the department took it. For the past several years, even that activity no longer occurs due to changes in a graduate curriculum that has "no room for it." In recent years, several thousand people in North America attended videoconferences I conducted on teaching issues in conjunction with the Tidewater Consortium on Higher Education. My department was one of the "campus sponsors" of the program. One colleague attended.

Recently, another asked if I would donate a copy of my book *Teaching With Style* to a resource area for our graduate students who would be teaching courses (i.e., at this moment in time doing so largely without supervision and training) or making presentations. "I'll make sure I indicate that I asked you to do this and the reason your book is there is because of my request," my colleague responded. I think the concern was that if it were placed in the resource area without the note, someone might think my narcissism had gotten out of hand. Or, perhaps I was arrogant enough to think that the information actually might be helpful to someone.

Thus, there is some sensitivity, anxiety, envy, or something that prevails in a system when a member of that system develops a high profile in an area. Teaching is a very personal experience and thus any discussions about teaching methods get down to people at some level relating it to themselves. Thus, if I suggest, as gently as I can, that active learning processes have decided advantages over traditional methods, some will take that as an attack on what they do. What occurs normally in discussions at conferences and workshops about the advantages and disadvantages of teaching is sometimes seen as a threat when it occurs in your own backyard. It is almost as if you are pointing a finger at others and saying, "You are not good enough." This may not be the intent but it is what is sometimes heard.

I am actually pretty good at interpersonal communication and have published and taught people how to do such things. But with issues of teaching, conference and workshop participants as well as colleagues can become defensive. Possessing good skills in communicating ideas to others is not easy nor do such skills negate the defensiveness. In a conversation about such issues, one of my colleagues, a clinical psychologist, noted that changing teaching was almost like getting people to change their personalities. "Our teaching methods are part of how we define ourselves, [he noted] they are part of our self-image." If he's right, and I think he has a valid point, any suggestion about options and alternatives can be threatening. To make such comments effectively means that something new must be assimilated into the mental constructs that comprise our self-image. To do so, we often have to "let go" of something from our past to accommodate a new way of doing things. This is not easy.

I am reminded of the concept of a "positive addiction" here. Positive addictions are things that people do that seem to be helpful but are ultimately a crutch to help them deal with issues in their lives. Thus, someone exercises to a fault to manage anxiety over how they look. Or, they read self-help books constantly looking for ways to improve themselves. Such things are addictive because a dependency develops whereby the activity cannot be given up. Perhaps this is what happens when we get locked into patterns in teaching. Such things are over learned and overused but provide a sense of direction and purpose to our professional lives. In the process, they help us to deal with underlying issues of control and authority in those social structures we call classrooms. Instead of looking for alternative ways of how to teach as representing new ways to express our need for control and authority, they are perceived as a threat to established and familiar routines to do so. Thus, people become anxious and threatened by any suggestion that a change might be needed.

The bottom line is that no one involved in promoting options to current teaching practices will be universally accepted. What one hopes for is that people will at least listen and decide for themselves what is valuable about the suggestions made. What you don't want to have happen is for people to become defensive and thus not think that anything is of value. It is not easy to do so but across the populations of people I interact with on such issues I think I have been generally successful in this regard.

* * * * *

Tony Grasha was a Social Psychologist and a Professor of Psychology in the Department of Psychology at the University of Cincinnati. He served as Director of the University of Cincinnati's Institute of Research and Training in Higher Education and the University of Cincinnati's Faculty Resource Center. He served as the Executive Editor of the interdisciplinary journal *College Teaching*. Grasha was the first recipient of the Distinguished Teaching Professor at the University of Cincinnati and has won the AB Dolley Cohen Award for Excellence in University Teaching with his focus in aspects on enhancing the teaching/learning process, on teaching styles and student learning styles, and on curriculum and organizational issues in higher education. The American Psychological Association has recognized his achievements in teaching everyday applications of psychology. His publications in higher education include articles, chapters, coauthored books, and his recent work *Teaching with Style: A Practical Guide to Enhancing Learning by Understanding Teaching and Learning Styles*. A recent recognition award was the recipient of the Northeastern Division of the Society of Teachers of Family Medicine.

Chapter 5

Smiles, Laughter, and Tears: The Glue of Relationships and Learning

By Joseph Lowman

For me, attending a Lilly Conference on College Teaching always begins the same way. While working my way through the familiar landmarks of the Cincinnati International Airport, finding a small group of other academics also waiting for a ride—I wonder if members of other professional groups are so easy to spot—and being whisked through the barren November Midwestern landscape to Oxford and the Marcum Center, the physical sensations, initial conversations with others in the van, and private thoughts have had a remarkable similarity over the 18 years I have been attending regularly. Quite honestly, my thoughts on the hour's ride to Oxford include dread as well as eagerness, e.g. "I'm tired at this time in the fall semester and I have so many things to do at home; why did I decide to come again this year?" "I enjoy meeting new people but I hope some of my old friends will be there so I won't be lonely or have to spend the entire time talking with strangers" "I've always learned new and exciting things at Lilly but I'm afraid the presentations fail to excite me this year or offer much that is new." Walking up the steps of the Marcum Center is not unlike walking through the door of a college classroom for the first meeting of a term; it's a combination of positive and negative anticipations that are impressively similar year after year. As I look back on the intellectual and personal impact of the Lilly Conferences over the years, I see other similarities in this experience with that of the typical college course, a parallel that seems altogether fitting. Those similarities are the subject of this memoir.

What do I remember from the Lilly Conferences over the years? Not surprisingly, I remember many things I learned from preparing my own presentations, new ones most every year. However, I remember most vividly others' presentations—more specifically, I remember new topics that I heard about there for the first time (e.g. cooperative learning, teaching portfolios, using the world-wide web in teaching, collecting assessment data from students). Moreover, I remember presentations that made new connections among general concepts I was already familiar with or that suggested applications to new examples or problems more often than those that focused on brand new information. How could a psychologist ever forget Darbe Lewes' fresh and insightful application of reinforcement principles to college teaching using her amazing dog Folly? To be sure, the formal presentations I've participated in and attended at Lilly have been a big part of what I have learned at the conferences, but the best intellectual moments have been unexpected and not easily anticipated beforehand from the program.

The learning that occurs in and around our own college classes is not unlike my learning at Lilly Conferences. Most teachers would agree with the statement, "The best way to learn something really well is to teach it to someone else." All teachers learn new information and skills from class preparation, especially when expanding our offerings to include new topics and courses. Similarly, our students learn new information from our courses.

But like what I've gained from Lilly conferences, acquiring new ideas or skills is a limited objective when compared with other possible outcomes. Based on what my students have told me—and I know from conversations with colleagues that other teachers have heard the same thing—the learning that leaves the strongest impression is connections among existing knowledge, rather than isolated concepts or observations. Rarer and more lasting are the "Ah ha" experiences in which an overarching perspective on old ideas offers a whole new way of seeing the world or ourselves. Students report that sometimes it is a teacher's anecdote or illustrative example that triggers such insights; sometimes it is a phrase or idea presented in a reading, or an experience on a field trip, in a laboratory, or in an art or music studio. Sometimes it is the discussion after class as students continue talking among themselves in hallways, sidewalks, or coffee shops that leads to the higher order learning that is so valued over time. And yes, such moments also occur for students while interacting with the teacher.

Unfortunately for us instructors, it is difficult if not impossible to know how exactly to create such moments of higher order insight in our students. Sure, we can make these moments more likely by the use of complex and open-ended presentations of course content, by our pro-vocative discussions with students, and by the critical thinking we model in and outside of class, but such lasting insights are simply too personal and elusive to be achieved with regularity by any direct method. Like the early farmers who could only sow their seeds on rough ground and wait to see if and where the sprouts would appear, modern college teachers aiming for higher level objectives must largely be content with spreading a lot of potent ideas, fertilizing them with engaging examples, and hop-ing some of them have a transforming effect on our students.

Thus far, I've applied the basic traditional intellectual learning ob-jectives to my experiences as a teacher and participant at Lilly Confer-ences and shown how they are similar to the cognitive outcomes our students gain from our courses. Cognitive objectives are only the begin-ning, however, as the Lilly Conferences have also been for me the set-ting for numerous interpersonal encounters, many of them also meaningful.

Ask me to scan for my most salient memories of Lilly Conferences over the years and I'm most likely to think of personal encounters and relationships with other presenters and participants. Some of these were initiated in conversations on the rides to Oxford, some began over meals, some resulted from conversation with someone sitting beside me before a presentation, some from an encounter after one of my own presenta-tions with a participant in the audience (or between me and a speaker whose presentation I had just attended). Other encounters occurred in more social settings: the receptions, during meals, the sing-a-long ses-sions at the Miami Inn, the dances, the Readers' Theatre Productions in the evening, or simply while standing around during the breaks. What impresses me most about these personal encounters—many fleeting, some more lasting—is how comfortable and easy they typically were and how effortlessly many brief encounters lead to more involved and lasting re-lationships, a number of which have resulted in joint work and have spanned many years and Lilly Conferences. The easy camaraderie among most Lilly participants (including the presenters) likely results from our shared interest in and commitment to college teaching and our legitimate assumption that other participants will share these values. Occasionally, during my travels to various colleges around the country, I meet a faculty member strongly committed to teaching who reports feeling isolated and unappreciated on their home campus. My advice has always been the same: "If you want to meet people from a variety of disciplines who share your values about the importance of college teaching, attend one of the Lilly Conferences."

Some of my relationships with people I have met at Lilly have grown in intimacy and longevity even though our face-to-face contacts have been largely restricted to Oxford, Ohio, and our relationships maintained by occasional e-mail messages during the year. I have learned about their career plans, their families, and what makes them happy. With a few, I have grieved with them over their health problems, professional losses, and personal pain. With others I have celebrated their achievements (a new administrative challenge or publication, a move to a new location and job, a satisfying new personal interest or hobby). Whether relatively fleeting or enduring, the personal encounters I so strongly associate with Lilly demonstrates for me the importance of this human dimension of our professional lives.

Similarly, personal encounters are equally important to our professional work with students. The memories that stand out over 33 years as a college professor are most often specific encounters with students, encounters largely initiated by them. I think of the discouraged 35-year-old mother of two who transferred to my university from a two-year-old school and was so intimidated by the younger and more sophisticated students that her dream of a professional education was growing dimmer day by day. I recall the post-midnight phone call from a student saying she had just received a phone call from the police saying her finance had been killed and telling me she didn't think she could take our exam later in the day. I remember innumerable students who have come by to talk about mental health problems experienced by their friends or various members of their families. Similarly, I think of the large number of students who have sought me out as an informal advisor, as someone with whom to talk about their choice of major or career path or their fears about the less certain adult world awaiting them after school. I am confident my memories of student encounters are similar to those of other college instructors. To be sure, most of my personal relationships with students have been limited to their work in my class and to the months they took my course, but many others have become more intimate and endured for longer periods of time, sometimes for years after the students graduated.

Empirical studies of student and faculty memories support this emphasis on personal relationships as a context for learning (Lowman, 1995). Peter Giordano of Belmont University in Nashville, Tennessee has initiated a systematic study (2003) of student, alumni, and faculty memories and has identified the importance of what he calls "Critical Moments," many of which are personally transforming. These moments, typically unpredictable and powerful, have a life-long impact on the person's intellectual, personal, or professional development. Given the ubiquity and importance of these interpersonal encounters to classroom teaching and to a recurring professional conference like Lilly what are we to conclude about the role and the importance of this interpersonal dimension to teaching and learning across all settings?

I believe that for faculty and students alike, our work-related personal encounters and relationships provide an engaging, motivating, and reassuring matrix—or glue, if you will—within which our more objective and intellectual work (including learning) occurs. This interpersonal matrix is necessary for other work, even while being insufficient by itself. The Lilly Conference and our college classes are not exclusively interpersonal encounter groups. They are work arenas in which to think and to consider new ideas with sufficient effort and depth so as to create useful and lasting learning. But each setting is also undeniably an interpersonal context in which recognition of this truth and deliberate effort to encourage such relationships promotes morale, motivation, and, ultimately, learning. As my title suggests, I believe that the smiles of our initial encounters with one another and the laughter (and sometimes tears) that can follow as relationships are formed, bespeak the necessary role of interpersonal encounters in reaching the higher-order intellectual objectives and the transforming personal impact we associate with the best of college teaching.

Are my thoughts and emotions at the end of Lilly Conferences as similar as they are at the beginning? Yes. Invariably, I climb aboard the van headed for the Cincinnati airport with more energy than when I got off a few days before. My fears that the presentations would be boring or meaningless have never been fulfilled. I have always met new people and typically reconnected with old friends. Most importantly, I have always left Oxford reaffirmed in my own beliefs in the importance of what we college teachers do for a living. Professional and personal rejuvenation may be difficult for many to attain. For me, however, my participation over the years in the Lilly Conferences on College Teaching has consistently achieved this goal for me, largely through the positive human qualities of other participants and the personal atmosphere deliberately fostered. I walk out of every college class at the end of a term with the same warm glow in my chest that I have when leaving the Marcum Center at the end of Lilly Conference on College Teaching, and I know that the feeling comes from a common source: satisfying personal encounters.

References

Giordano, P. (2003). "Critical Moments in Learning: Do We Know When We Are Teaching?" W. Harold Moon Invited Address. Southeastern Conference on the Teaching of Psychology, Marietta, GA

Lowman, J. (1995). *Mastering the Techniques of Teaching* (2d ed.). San Francisco: Jossey-Bass.

* * * * *

A native of western North Carolina Joe Lowman is a graduate of Greensboro College and the University of North Carolina at Chapel Hill, where he received his Ph.D. in clinical psychology and is a Professor of Psychology. Throughout his 36-year academic career at UNC-CH Joe has regularly taught undergraduates as well as graduate students and his inspirational teaching has been recognized several times with departmental and university-wide teaching awards. Since publishing *Mastering the Techniques of Teaching* in 1984 (2d ed. 1995), Joe's research has focused on exemplary college instructors and ways to promote it among college faculty. He is an active consultant with universities and corporations around the country on ways to promote high quality instruction using a mix of tradition and technology-based techniques. Currently, Joe is also studying various topics in the field of evolutionary personality. Next to teaching, Lowman's passions are playing tuba with several local groups, including the Triangle Tuba Quartet, and singing bass in his church choir.

Chapter 6

Teaching as a Human Event

By Barbara J. Millis

I recently heard a talk on "Teaching and Leading" given by Brig Gen (Ret) Mal Wakin. He was speaking to 148 new and returning faculty at the U. S. Air Force Academy during faculty orientation. Many of his points resonated with me. But one of his opening ones really struck home. He said that if you are a truly great teacher, it is still doubtful that down the road your students will remember much of what you "taught them." But, your students will remember YOU. I don't know how many of my students do remember me, but my head started reeling with all the students that *I* remember after a teaching career spanning almost three decades. Ironically, only a handful stand out, but each one of them made a indelible impression on me—often for better or for worse—and all of them taught me important things about being a teacher and about being a human being.

Joe Lowman, in *Mastering the Techniques of Teaching*, focuses on the classroom as a dramatic arena in which human beings interact. I totally agree with this image. My interactions with students began when I was a young, extremely nervous teaching assistant (TA) teaching freshman (Yes! We were sexist in the 60's despite bra-burning women libbers!) composition at Florida State University. Two students come to mind. The first made a comment to me about midway through the course, "Gee, Miss Baker. I really appreciate how nicely you dress for this class." I was floored because this remark totally shattered the image I carried of myself as a dowdy graduate student wearing only one pair of high-heeled shoes (beige ones issued to me as a tour guide at the GE Pavilion at the 1965 New York World's Fair). From that off-hand comment, I learned that students do not always view me through the lens I hold up. Often, they will have a far more positive opinion. The second student gave me the gift of self-confidence. She invited me to her sorority house to be honored as an "Apple Teacher." I attended the ceremony with tears in my eyes. I had graduated in three years and my former college room-mate was now a senior at this same sorority. Sitting at the head table with a large apple placemat, I was being singled out as a professional in my field: that early—very kind—acknowledgement set me on the path to being the best teacher I could possibly be.

From Florida State I went on to the challenges of teaching adult learners in open enrollment classes at Kirkwood Community College. Again, two students stood out. One was a struggling, semi-literate male student from a lower socio-economic background. One day during an informal exchange on the campus, Joe* turned to my husband and said, "Hey, tell your old lady to give me an 'A' in her class." I was stunned by his apparent rudeness—"civility" was not then the issue it is now—and hurt by the apparent far-from-professional image he held of me. Only later did I realize that Joe simply didn't have the linguistic tools to carry on an appropriate conversation. The term "old lady" was perfectly acceptable in the pool halls he frequented: how could he intuit the negative impact such a reference had on me? I know that Joe did not emerge from my composition class with the tools he needed, but I came out with a new awareness that students will bring all kinds of baggage into the classroom—often unconscious, culturally derived baggage. It is our job to see beyond that baggage and to reach—if we can—the person underneath. The second student, Duc, was a young Vietnam refugee eager to share his culture in a strange land. (Iowa's sloping plains and harsh winters must have been particularly strange!) He learned of my husband's interest in international cooking and of his service in Vietnam in the U.S. Army. He insisted on coming to our apartment to teach us how to make Vietnamese egg rolls. As a point of pride, although we knew he was very poor, he would accept no money for the extensive ingredients he brought that day. Duc's satisfaction came in seeing my husband's clumsy fingers fold the delicate wrappers and in watching us consume with delight our first-ever Vietnamese egg rolls. From this experience, I learned to value the gifts that students gladly share with their teachers, many of them far removed from academia.

When my husband and I flew to Tokyo in 1978 to join the Asian Division of the University of Maryland University College, another series of academic adventures—and life lessons—began. During this wonderful opportunity to teach enlisted personnel and their family members on far-flung military installations throughout Asia (Korea, Japan, including Okinawa, Guam, and the Philippines), I encountered the best students I have ever met. No, they were not the "brightest," merely the "best" because they were so motivated. Many of my students had joined the military because it offered their only avenue to a college education. They were *so* grateful to be taking classes on top of their military obligations. Two in particular stand out in Asia. I remember well a young African-American airman who struggled in my "Introduction to Composition" course. One day he submitted a paper that clearly deserved a failing grade. I disliked awarding failing grades in any case, but like all conscientious teachers, I felt the need to uphold "standards." But, I couldn't just slap an "F" on this particular paper because shining through the semi-literate prose was a beautiful paean to Leroy's wife. I met one-on-one with Leroy, trying to explain the difference between a grade based on a writing product as opposed to a grade based on the content. In my clumsy way, I tried to encourage him to revise and to continue to celebrate the depth of his love. The final result was still only a "D," but I hope to this day that he recognized how much I respected him as a human being even though I couldn't reward him for his writing skills. I learned, of course, that students bring not only cultural "baggage," but emotional baggage as well. We need to nurture the human being beneath our sometimes sterile assignments. The second student was the exact opposite of Leroy: a remarkably talented writer. Dell, in fact, went on to become an acclaimed novelist and film consultant. I rarely give "A-pluses" but Dell earned one with a humorous causal analysis paper dealing with faulty toilet bowl detonators. Dell was also an exuberant party-goer who sometimes let the "US Marine" element of his personality gain the upper hand. At an end-of-semester party my husband and I gave for our adult students at our apartment on Okinawa, Dell showed up after an office party already pretty under the influence. Before long, he was showing our horrified guests his military war wounds, which necessitated an action more commonly known as "dropping trou'"). At that point, Dell's Marine wife, Margie left in disgust. (Margie, we learned later, was jettisoned after Dell started climbing the Hollywood ladder.) Dell then turned his attention to the other ladies at the party and managed to infuriate Matt by his unwelcome attentions to his wife. Desperate to avoid the pending flight, I remember clutching Matt with all my might, feeling his tense body triggered to explode into violence. I kept whispering, "Matt, he's drunk. He doesn't know what he's doing. Please don't start a fight. Please don't wreck our apartment." Matt—bless him!—backed off, and my husband managed to convince Dell to climb into the backseat of the car with him for the drive home. The driver, a female Maryland teacher who fortunately had a sense of humor and a humane perspective, merely whooped as Dell periodically leaned forward to grab protruding parts of her anatomy. When the trio finally located Dell's off-base apartment, my husband semi-carried him to the door where he fumbled for a key and managed to fling open the door to face the family dog. The startled beagle gave Dell a disgusted look and proceeded to back away! I'm not certain what I learned from this student . . . I guess it was to value the experiences—however unexpected—to which our students bring us.

I continued to teach adult learners when we resumed stateside careers with the University of Maryland University College. One of my favorite classes was an open-learning one on critical thinking. With optional attendance because most of the work was done—pre-WWW—at a distance, I met regularly with a small core of students who preferred, as I did, the face-to-face conversations. And, they were deep and rich conversations spawned by the divergent viewpoints of students such as a male African-American, a Hispanic female, and a white single mother whose two sons faced the prejudices of a mixed marriage. We explored a myriad of topics and I—and these special students—emerged the wiser for the course. Thus, I was unprepared for a session on critical thinking at a professional conference where a Black man rose and stated emphatically—and unchallenged—that no White teacher could ever teach thinking skills to a Black person. I was reeling, but I never lost my conviction that something magical had happened in that stimulating class. That was a lesson I will always remember. My favorite class was a junior-level survey class on Children/Adolescent Literature. A range of students attended, from English majors seeking an "easy A" to a Vietnamese daycare worker who wanted to read good literature to her charges. Anh struggled in that course because her language skills were limited, but by this time I had discovered the power of cooperative learning, and she was safely supported in a permanent learning team by three other adults who made certain that she was able to earn a legitimate "C" in the course. On the end-of-course student evaluations I recognized Anh's handwriting. She wrote simply, "In this class I have found true friends." I learned through this the power of structured group work because it enables human beings to reach out to others in meaningful ways. Another student in that class, a 30ish female, seemed totally self-sufficient, although she, too, was a contributing team member. Only near the end of the semester did I catch a glimpse of her personal demons as her purse slipped open to reveal an unmistakable pint of gin. I never followed up with this student—I didn't know how—but I understood suddenly that we can never fully understand the complexity of our students and their tangled lives.

After I accepted a position at the U. S. Air Force Academy (USAFA), I faced for the first time traditional-age students. Given my age, they were more challenging in many ways than my adult learners. I quickly learned that although these students were bright, their composition skills were also all over the map. Virtually all of them were motivated not to read *Hamlet* or *A Farewell to Arms*, but to fly airplanes. At least one frustrated cadet, a physics major, accused me—respectfully, of course, with an extra "ma'am" thrown in—of fabricating all this esoteric symbolism. Only one student during my seven years at USAFA took the time to act on a genuine interest in literature. Even though I could never convince Bill to become an English major, I treasured his requests for books by James Joyce and William Faulkner even two years after our sophomore literature course had ended. Our subsequent discussions were a joy. Thus, I cheered with extra enthusiasm as I watched Bill accept his diploma, knowing that he would be an exemplary officer. I learned that some students will remain intellectually curious despite the demands on their time. I am certain, also, that such curiosity manifests itself in a range of academic disciples and out-of-class experiences. Another student was far less successful. In fact, he was a plagiarist in an institution that prides itself on a robust honor code. Michael was a student so enthusiastic—perhaps impulsive, in retrospect—that during a carefully structured debate on *Antigone* (four teams debating "Should Antigone have buried her brother?" and "Should Creon be impeached for poor leadership?"), he leapt up and joined the rebuttal of another team. I really liked him. But, just as I was experiencing the devastation of a beloved mother-in-law dying of cancer, I found clear evidence that Michael had plagiarized an essay from a WWW source. I then saw evidence of plagiarism in another essay. I finally discovered that Michael had lifted verbatim from the Web his entire research paper. I invested enormous amounts of emotional energy and time preparing evidence, testifying, and soul-searching. It took months for the case to be resolved, thanks to the safeguards of a carefully constructed cadet-run honor system, but I learned that justice will prevail if we are committed to the process. I also learned that we can never know what is in the hearts and minds of our students. I was seated next to Michael at the formal honor board hearing and during a recess, I turned to him and asked what he had done during the break. He broke into an infectious smile and told me about his trip back home. He was not a bad kid; his plagiarism was likely driven by desperation and had nothing to do with me as a human being.

Being a human being makes us committed teachers. It makes us love our students even as they confound us, inspire us, and give us grief. It makes us strive to know them as people even as we can never really know them. It makes us want to be, as I decided after my first year as a TA, the best teachers we can be. I want always to remain an "Apple Teacher."

*All names are deliberately fictitious.

* * * * *

Barbara J. Millis is the Director of the Excellence in Teaching Program, University of Nevada at Reno and formally Director of Faculty Development at the U.S. Air Force Academy. She received her Ph.D. in English literature from Florida State University. The former Assistant Dean of Faculty Development at the University of Maryland University College, she frequently offers workshops at various colleges/ universities and professional conferences. Publications have included articles in cooperative learning, classroom observations, the teaching portfolio, micro teaching, syllabus construction, peer review and focus groups, and co-authored the books *Cooperative Learning for Higher Education Faculty* and *Using Simulations to Promote Learning in Higher Education*. In 1998, she received the U.S. Air Force Academy's prestigious McDermott Award for Research Excellence in the Humanities and Social Sciences and the Outstanding Educator Award. After the Association of American Colleges and Universities selected the Air Force Academy as a leadership institution, she began serving in 2001 as a liaison to the AAC&U's Greater Expectations Consortium on Quality Education.

Chapter 7

A Lucky Series of Events

By Craig E. Nelson

A series of lucky events has shaped my journey from wanting to study amphibians and retiles to wanting to be an effective teacher and, later, a student of alternative modes of teaching. Each twist in the path has led me to dig deeper into the teaching challenges it brought forth. Twists included (in this sequence): a Woodrow Wilson graduate fellowship (focused on preparing teachers), an early unplanned encounter with Perry's work on cognitive development, a demonstration showing that effective group work could be done even in large classes, tenure with teaching as the area of excellence, a Lilly Postdoctoral Teaching Fellowship (I fortuitously included tenured faculty in these), a shift of part of my teaching to environmental science, attendance by a conference organizer at my first contributed paper on teaching, a subsequent long series of invitations to give presentations at conferences and national meetings and at individual institutions, invitations to prepare chapters on teaching, choice as a Carnegie Scholar, and a national award. Teaching challenges/ responses (again in sequence) included: organizing my first courses as a faculty member, redoing my own thinking and my ideas of teaching in response to Perry's ideas, integrating Perry with structures group work, serious evaluation and revision of my teaching principles under guidance of the Lilly program, striving to understand the complexity of environmental issues, the role learning to do workshops for other faculty and interacting extensively with them in further refining my ideas, writing the chapters, learning to interact more effectively with other nascent scholars of teaching, and (currently) trying to learn how to foster change in my home institution. This chapter traces the complex interplay of the lucky events with the challenges and my responses to them. In passing it illustrates the large role of serendipity in a complex career, the value of tenure and the freedom it confers, and the multiple seasons of a faculty member's life.

* * * * *

Craig Nelson is a professor of Biology at Indiana University and is a Carnegie Scholar. He has taught diverse courses in biology, intensive freshman seminars, great books and other honors classes, several collaboratively taught interdisciplinary courses and he regularly teaches a graduate course on "Alternative Approaches to Teaching College Biology." His SOTK papers address critical thinking and mature valuing, diversity, active learning, teaching evaluation, and genres of Sot. His awards include several for distinguished teaching, the President's Medal for Excellence at Indiana University and Outstanding Research and Doctoral University Professor of the Year 2000 (Carnegie/CASE).

Chapter 8

Upside Down Learning

By Gail Rice

How excited I was to be giving my very first lecture! The topic was "Cesarean Birth" and my class was a group of 45 junior nursing students at the University of Illinois College of Nursing. I wanted to be prepared as well as possible, so I went to the library and read everything that I could find on the subject. Then I prepared a hefty outline and started fitting in all of the information. I spent so much time with the detailed handout that I had no time for audiovisual aids, other than an old 16 mm film I would show at the end of the lecture. Some of my recollections of that memorable afternoon:

- No time for the film (big mistake when it was listed on the handout)
- Rushing through my notes as I tried to talk about everything I had written down
- Frustrated and then bored looks on the part of the students (and eventually even my faculty colleagues)

The subject was so exciting to me that it was hard for me to realize that I had overloaded everyone in the room.

I had never wanted to be a teacher. In fact, I specifically chose to go into the medical field, so as to avoid any form of teaching. Most professional educators can tell you about an outstanding educational experience they had as a child. That experience, they would go on to say, encouraged them to aspire to being an educator themselves. Not me. I had attended a one-room and then a two-room school, where the largest number of students in the same grade was 4. I would work independently on my daily assignments, finishing them midmorning and then spending the rest of my school day reading library books about horses and cowboys. Occasionally my teacher would ask me to help the younger students. Of course, I did not welcome these "teaching opportunities," as they took me away from my beloved books, which, although they were certainly not classics or anything resembling great literature, whisked me away from a boring schoolroom to an exciting world. It seemed to me that any learning that I achieved during those early formative years was more of an accident than the result of any great teaching I had experienced. I guess I learned enough in elementary school, although I had no idea how this had happened. Certainly I learned from those early years that teaching had no draw for me.

I graduated from a high school class of 80 students where sports and work received more attention than academics and where there were no advanced placement courses and nothing more demanding than second-year algebra (my favorite subject). Again, I experienced no "great" teachers or wonderful learning experiences. In those days, most girls who went on to college chose between nursing, teaching, and secretarial training—since I didn't want to be a teacher and since everyone in my family was either a doctor or a nurse, I chose nursing.

It was quite a surprise for me to discover early in my nursing education that good nurses were good teachers. I quickly noticed that it did little good to help patients recover from the present illness without teaching them how to live healthier lives, in order to avoid future illnesses. My role models during those nursing school days, I discovered, were not only the nurse educators on the university faculty, but also the nurses on the hospital floor, in the outpatient offices, and in the public health clinics, who were teaching and motivating—not only the patients, but also patients' families, staff members, other health professionals, and the student nurses. To be a good nurse, I discovered, I would have to know much more than all of the clinical science, pathophysiology, biochemistry, and physics that made up what I perceived to be the important part of the medical curriculum. I would have to know a lot about psychology, health behavior change, motivation, and learning, as well.

And, so I began to find this new science fascinating. The first thing I did after graduating with a bachelor's degree in nursing was to enroll in a graduate program in educational psychology. Teaching was not my goal at that time. I just wanted to be a better nurse.

It wasn't until graduate school that I began to glimpse what a privilege it is to be taught well. I was working full time, taking care of two young children, and taking a full load of graduate classes when I enrolled in a class taught by Mr. Butler. By this time, I had studied quite a bit about teaching and learning, but I think this was really my first real *experience* in teaching and learning. Mr. Butler started each lecture by listing on the board exactly what he hoped we would be able to do by the end of the session. He taught, using examples and interactive exercises, slowly and methodically. He creatively designed activities, which required the students to revisit each important concept a number of times in different ways. When he had completed a particular objective, he would go to the board, eraser in hand, look at the students, and ask "Can I erase this one?" I didn't realize how thoroughly I had learned the material in Mr. Butler's course until the end of the term when I pulled out my books and notes, ready to spend a good portion of the night preparing for the final examination. I couldn't believe it! I already knew everything I needed to know for the exam. After a very short review, I got a good night of sleep, something pretty unheard of during those hectic graduate school examination weeks, and "cooled" the test.

Graduate school must have had an effect on my passion for good teaching. I think I first realized this when I got a traffic ticket for sliding through a stop sign. I figured that I should attend traffic school in order to keep the ticket off my driving record, so I started "shopping" for my required 8 hours of traffic education. I found myself interrogating the persons who answered the phone for the various traffic schools. "Who is the instructor? May I talk to the instructor about the class? What are the instructor's qualifications—not only in the topic area, but what does he know about how to teach? Is he going to bore us to death? What are the objectives for the course? What will I be able to do as a result of taking this course, other than get the citation removed from my record?" I finally found a course taught for busy professors—it was a private course, which took less than an hour. I found I could endure poor teaching, as long as it didn't last too long.

My husband, also a university professor, and I began to get really passionate about a person's "right" for good learning when our 15-year-old son started losing interest in his schoolwork and his grades began to drop. Forcing a young man to leave his friends for the last 12 years in the middle of his junior year in high school and to cross town 25 miles to attend another private school with different teachers and students in the hope of rekindling the joy of learning may have been a desperate move, but we felt that it was worth whatever it took. Good learning is one of life's most priceless possibilities.

Good learning is not always easy to come by. Even after finishing a doctoral degree in education, I still was somewhat "in the dark" about what constitutes good teaching and learning. Looking back, I think I may have learned more over the years from my students and clients than I did from much of my own formal learning. I taught at three different universities for six different "schools" or departments. In addition, I taught courses for expectant parents—more than 7,000 women and their families enrolled over an 18-year period. So I have had a good many students contribute to my learning about teaching.

What have I learned? My students have taught me that they learn more and they learn it better when . . .

- Learning is truly active
- Learners are ready to learn
- Learners are having fun
- The teacher loves the subject
- The teacher gives up the lectern
- The teacher is creative
- Experiences precede theory and application
- Teachers look for (and expect) the best in students
- Students know that the teacher cares about them
- The teacher designs the learning period with educational psychology principles in mind

What do my present students think about my teaching? They often write on their course evaluation forms things like, "Thanks for making the time fly," "Thanks for making the learning easy," or "Thanks for making learning fun." I consider these comments the ultimate compliments. When I am asked what has contributed to my approach to teaching, I would have to list some of the following.

Organizations (and conferences) like Creative Training Techniques, American Society for Training and Development, Kansas State University Higher Education Programs, The Lilly Conferences on Higher Education, The International Society for Enhancing Teaching and Learning have boosted my understanding of what goes into good learning experiences. Some big influencers include:

- Charles Bonwell and James Eison's lectures, workshops, and book on Active Learning
- Michele Deck and Dave Arch's workshops
- Dave Meier's Accelerated Learning workshops and book

Where has all of this "learning" led me? What is different? I call it "Upside-Down Teaching." Recently I helped some graduate public health students plan a learning session for a small group of middle-aged Hispanic patients. Their objective was to encourage the patients to increase physical activity in their daily lives. These graduate students were planning to teach their patient session a lot like I planned for that cesarean birth lecture 30 years ago. The student teachers had thoroughly researched the topic of physical exercise. They had even looked up some internet materials on the topic of cultural attitudes about exercise in this specific ethnic group. They had developed posters, overhead transparencies, and handouts listing the benefits of regular physical exercise. In spite of all of their preparations, they had a deep concern that their teaching would not make a bit of difference to this group of patients—and with good reason. All of their previous efforts with similar topics and similar clients had seemed pretty futile.

These students had just attended a graduate seminar I had given on the topic of "Upside-Down Teaching," so they made an appointment to try to get some help.

I asked the group two questions. "How could you start the session with an experience, instead of theory," I asked. "And then, how could you help the participants integrate the ideas into their own lives?" Pretty soon, they were all talking at once and, as their excitement rose, the teaching/learning plan began to fall into place. The session would start with a lively version of musical chairs and end with participants filling out a little commitment card that would be mailed back to each of them in 3 weeks.

I looked forward to hearing back from the student group. They came to my office a couple of weeks later to tell me what had happened. They described the laughter and exuberance as the group of patients walked around in two circles in opposite directions while music was playing. When the music stopped, they were to find their partner from the other circle, grab both hands, and squat together. If they were the last ones to get together and squat, they got a point. But, unlike musical chairs, they were not out of the game. They had to keep going. After about five minutes of this, everyone was ready to sit down. There were prizes for all of the participants. One couple was particularly slow at squatting together; they received the "booby" prize for the couple with the most points. The student leader began to ask the group to describe how they felt after the physical activity. Pretty soon everyone was remarking about how good, relaxed, more comfortable, etc. they felt now as a result of the exercise.

After talking together about the benefits of exercise, the participants were able to identify a number of things that make it hard for them to exercise regularly. The group talked together about things like unsafe neighborhoods to walk alone in and not being able to afford exercise equipment or gym memberships. Then the group, not the teachers, came up with some pretty creative solutions. " I couldn't believe it," one of the student teachers exclaimed. " Three of the women who live close to each other are going to walk together in the mornings." "I can hardly imagine that happening if we had taken our usual approach to teaching this class," another of the students exclaimed.

The leaders finished the session by asking each participant to fill in a postcard, which said:

> "This is what I am going to do tomorrow to exercise. . .
>
> This is what I am going to continue to do for the next three weeks . . ."

Participants then addressed the other side of the card to themselves and were told that these cards would be mailed to them in three weeks, so they would not forget their commitment to get more exercise into their daily routines.

As the group of students left my office, one of them stayed behind. "I didn't realize how important teaching is in this profession," he said. I didn't think I wanted to be a teacher, so I decided to get my master's degree in public health. I had no idea that teaching could be such a kick."

Ingrid Hoffmann, a visiting professor at Loma Linda University Fall 2002, on leave from her position in Nutrition Ecology in Germany, was ready to take her teaching to a new level. One day she called for an appointment to talk about teaching. Ingrid is one of those enthusiastic people who brings out your best, so it wasn't long until we were swapping stories of magical moments in the classroom. A few weeks later, she stopped by again. "I have to tell you about a lecture I gave last week," she said as she walked into my office, her face glowing. "I especially remembered one thing you told me the last time we talked. You said, 'Don't start with a lot of theory. Instead, start your teaching with an experience.'"

I hadn't remembered being so prescriptive, but I was interested to hear what she had to say. "Last week," she continued, "I had agreed to give the lecture for the School of Public Health's Dean's Seminar so I attended the week before to get an idea of what the seminar was like. The previous week's teacher could not have been more boring as he tried to discuss epidemiology while the students ate their lunches, talked out loud to each other, displayed no interest in the lecture, took no notes, and got up and left while the speaker was still talking. I could see I was in for a real challenge."

"My topic was nutrition—particularly how do you get the recommended number of servings of fruit and vegetables into your day. I knew I had to follow your advice," she told me,"but I kept wondering how I could start with an experience—and then I had it! The students would be eating while I talked—I would let that be the experience. I found out ahead of time what food would be served that day. I had the students figure out what they were eating right then and how much more they would need to get their minimum requirements.

Ingrid went on to describe several times when the students laughed, which delighted her. She described the students as alive and animated. "No one went to sleep. No one left early." I wanted to comment that for a teacher, this is the ultimate compliment, but I couldn't get a word in edgewise. "I gave a quiz and passed out fruit as the awards, which the students loved. It was just a blast. I had no idea teaching could be such a high."

Ingrid was right. I can think of nothing more rewarding and more fun than teaching.

* * * * *

Dr. Gail Rice is responsible for faculty development at Loma Linda University, a health science campus located in Southern California. Her graduate degrees are in educational psychology and higher educational administration and leadership. Gail's undergraduate work was in nursing and public health education. She serves on numerous editorial boards for professional journals and boards for professional societies. She is a student of adult learning in many settings. She taught prenatal education courses to more than 14,000 clients. In addition, she has held professional positions at four universities in seven schools or department. Gail is presently teaching several on-line courses, but the classroom remains her "magic time" where she continually experiments to find ways to enhance learning for students and fellow faculty.

Chapter 9

Do Not Go Gently

By Laurie Richlin, Ph.D.

I am driven by ignorance. I don't like it. I am against people being put into situations where they could succeed if they had knowledge and they may fail without it. When people look at my Curriculum Vitae they wonder what the connection is between teaching LaMaze Childbirth Preparation and Early Parenting (which I did in the early 1970s) to teaching in and directing a Preparing Future Faculty program (which I do now). The way I see the connection is that parenthood and the professoriate are two of the most important professions there are—and they both suffer from lack of information provided to novices.

What drives my heart in the "teaching and learning business" is the business itself—how people initiate and succeed in academic careers. I am most concerned with the transition from "T.A. to tenure"—from graduate school to full membership in the academic community. (Okay, I also am interested in the revitalization of tenured faculty through the scholarly approach to teaching, but that is not my great love.) How do students make that transition? How do students who have come to graduate school to study the subjects they care about—and who were selected because of their abilities in those subjects—transform into people who can share what Shulman calls "disciplinary content knowledge" with students who probably do not have either their interest or ability in the field?

I currently am the director of a program that prepares graduate students for academic careers. How did I get here? It has been a long road, and was motivated—at least in part—by my own academic failures. In 1960 I was part of an experiment by Clark Kerr to build a small, residential, liberal arts college as part of the University of California system. Along with other selected students I was sent to the new Riverside campus. This was only a few years post-Sputnik. Through a combination of all of us young people "finding" each other, the headiness of the 1960s, and the teaching styles of the recent doctoral graduates who had been hired as our professors, approximately 40 percent of the entering students (including me) failed out (and this went on for successive cohorts each year for many years). The mismatch between the seminar-type teaching in college and the lack of critical thinking education during our (pre-Sputnik) grammar and high school years, led to an incompatibility resulting in failure to learn. How could we be expected to function at a developmental level necessary to apply, integrate, and evaluate knowledge when we barely comprehended the facts and figures of the world around us? Most of us entering freshmen were deep in the dualistic Perry stage of development. We had come just to be told. And our professors not only had not been educated to understand the cognitive development of college students or how various teaching methods enabled students to learn, they had not been educated to focus on learning at all.

I spent the year following my freshman failure at an amazing community college, where the professors challenged the students in ways and at levels that helped us grow. But when I reentered the University of California (at a different campus), I found the same lack of connection between the professors' assumptions and the students' cognitive abilities. Once again, I failed out.

Over the next two decades I took courses at prestigious universities (e.g., Chicago and Northwestern), community colleges (in California and Maryland), and schools everywhere I lived. Then, after 21 years of off-and-on undergraduate study I finally chose a major: political science. I completed two full-time years at a large, urban, state university and then, at the age of 40, I entered graduate school. My graduate interest was the study of higher education, which fit Mark Twain's observation that "the politics are so vicious because the stakes are so low." I became interested in how people became professors and, when I found out that graduate students were expected to make the leap from learner to professor without any preparation, I became fascinated with that transition. had been told in graduate courses that not only was there nothing known about teaching and learning in higher education, there were no faculty members interested in the subject. Wrong. It was at this time that I discovered (in the Chronicle of Higher Education) and attended the Lilly Conference on College Teaching at Miami University in Oxford, Ohio. it was in its 8th year, with several hundred participants discussing applications of theories of learning, challenges of active learning, and a plethora of other topics. One of the first sessions I attended was a report by faculty members from Alverno College about cognitive development of women college students, based on substantive research, and directly impacting how their students were taught. Other important sessions that year included research on encouraging student writing, presented by a national expert, and several seminars on good practices for preparing teaching assistants to teach.

I was enchanted with the idea that there was hidden knowledge that could have made possible a better connection between how the professors "taught" during my first year in college and my learning. The founder of the Lilly Conference was interested in expanding the Lilly concept, and less than a year-and-a-half later I, too, was directing a regional conference on college and university teaching, the first of 49 I have directed in California, New Hampshire, Massachusetts, Maryland, South Carolina, Georgia, Michigan, Texas, and Oregon. It was also at this time we began the Journal on Excellence in College Teaching, published by Miami University to provide a written forum for the scholarship of teaching in a peer reviewed, multidisciplinary journal.

All of this coincided with another project of mine. It turned out that at my graduate school there was an annual prize for the outstanding higher education student and it required an internship experience. I wanted to win the prize. I called the local university and asked whether they had any use for an intern who was interested in how the school prepared its teaching assistants (T.A.s). They had never heard of anyone being interested in that, but, indeed, they were in the process of developing a T.A. Training Program and would be interested in my coming out there and working with them. (By one of those wild chances in life, this was the University of California, Riverside campus, where I had first entered college 23 years before.)

I knew nothing about teaching, learning, teaching assistants, or, even, university life, outside of my own studies (which, to be sure, included a far greater number of campuses than most people have been on). Because my graduate school was freestanding and had no undergraduate population to experiment upon, up to this time I had never actually taught college students. Understandably, it was therefore a challenge to design a new program intended to immediately help the T.A.s teach their courses effectively as well as to prepare them for their future academic careers. It was in some ways luck that I did not know then what was "supposed" to be done, so I worked from the theories I had studied in the higher education program. To implement my program, I wrote and was awarded a national grant to put my theories into operation.

My operating theory was that I thought it was important for the new instructors to understand where their campus fit into the world of higher education institutions. What was the mission of the specific university they were at now? What were the missions of the institutions where they would apply for positions in the future? What were the purposes of their school's general education and departmental majors? I reasoned T.A.s should study teaching alongside T.A.s from many disciplines, taking advantage of ideas from across the curriculum. Moreover, they should know how students' cognitive abilities develop and how students actually learn. Finally, I thought they should know about aspects of the courses they were to teach.

To pull this information together, we developed a large, 3-ring notebook with the latest information on group learning, giving lectures, dealing with "diversity," and other issues. But there was no through-line (as actors need to have) behind the information.

I left that internship to write my dissertation, but was whisked away to develop a new faculty development program with four small colleges in the Midwest, funded by a two-year national grant. There was no reason to expect that I could do this. At that time, one's credibility needed to be established through many years of teaching experience before attempting to work with faculty about their own teaching. What did I have to offer? Well, I had ideas and I had literature. The practice of faculty development was becoming a profession that could depend on research into the teaching > < learning connection instead of reflection on individual practice. By focusing on helping the faculty focus on their students' learning needs, I was able to develop a self-sustaining program that the colleges involved could manage on their own after the grant was over.

At this point, in the early 1990's, the landmark book, Scholarship Reconsidered (Boyer 1990), was published. Ernie Boyer, the author, provided his draft of the manuscript to me so that I could use the template in my dissertation research. Using the four scholarships of discovery, integration, application, and teaching, my research looked at types of doctoral dissertation scholarship that were acceptable to graduate departments and were preferred by hiring institutions. Although the first three concepts were well described, the concept of the "scholarship of teaching" in that book and the subsequent Scholarship Reassessed (cite) was highly flawed. I began work at that time to differentiate between scholarly teaching (Richlin 1993) and the scholarship of teaching and to incorporate both into my work with current and future faculty members.

With this as my focus, I then spent two postdoctoral years with Gene Rice, at Antioch College, doing some institutional research on that special institution and publishing my dissertation research (Richlin 1993). I then took the position of director of the Office of Faculty Development at the University of Pittsburgh, where I had responsibility for the teaching practices of over 2,000 T.A.s and 4,200 faculty members (60 percent of them medical faculty). Leaving working with faculty mostly to my Associate Director, Brenda Manning, I developed and taught a course that was required of all T.A.s who would be teaching independently for the first time. Bringing together our experiences, Brenda and I became involved in the development of teaching portfolios and the evaluation of teaching through materials and observation. We wrote a curriculum (Improving a Teaching/Learning Evaluation System 1995) that would lead people to develop and bring together and reflect on their teaching materials before negotiating with their colleagues about how to evaluate teaching in their departments. For several years we worked with faculty members from various campuses to implement the system and develop their evaluation systems.

Brenda provided me with the key to making the teaching > < learning process efficient as well as effective. Her focus on learning objectives—and her insistence that we have them for every aspect of our work and the book—has made the greatest difference in what I can do to aid instructors in their quest for their students' learning. The sheer logic of translating teaching goals (such as those found in Angelo & Cross 199?) into learning objectives that can be seen and measured, and thereby used for evaluating student learning, makes the process as straightforward as it can be. By using learning objectives that are based on the characteristics of the professor (such a teaching style, personality, expertise), the students (such as cognitive development stage, interest in the subject, preparation), the content (such as course level, background needed), and the environment (such as time of day, noise and heat, room setup), a course can be designed to maximize the teaching > < learning interaction.

By this time I was directing seven regional Lilly conferences a year, teaching the T.A. courses on a half-time basis, and reviewing hundreds of proposals and manuscripts on the scholarship of teaching submitted to the conferences and to the Journal on Excellence in College Teaching. I moved from Pittsburgh back to Southern California and began, half time, the Preparing Future Faculty Program at my graduate alma mater. When that became a full- time position, the school was able to become part of a Miami University FIPSE project to develop Faculty Learning Communities (FLC) involving faculty members from our local undergraduate institutions with the graduate students interested in faculty careers. The FLC's have broadened the graduate students' perspectives by engaging with current faculty members on special topics in teaching.

What have I learned? Most important, I believe that instructors make many good, but implicit, professional decisions as they plan courses and teach their students. In order to help their students learn better, faculty members need to get to know themselves as teachers. They need to identify their values and goals. They need to make their decisions explicit. And, they need to give up old ideas about teaching such as "good teaching is generic," "teaching is a private matter," and "nobody knows what good teaching is."

I believe good teaching is highly individualized and context-dependent. Learning objectives must be based on the qualities, abilities, and interests of the professor, the students, the content, and the environment. No two courses, even with the same title or professor, will ever be the same. This individualized teaching takes place in an organizational context and must reflect the authentic values, beliefs, and goals of the organization it serves at all levels, from department to entire institution. Teaching is a public and community activity. And we do know what good teaching is, as well as how to continue to improve as teachers.

Over the past 15 years most of my teaching has been outside of classrooms. In all cases my efforts have been to make available knowledge—particularly vocabulary and structure—about Scholarly Teaching and about the Scholarship of Teaching and Learning for people who otherwise would not have access to that information. The biggest task, and where I begin, is helping faculty members realize that they have objectives for their students' learning and to help them make those objectives explicit. I find the process similar to untangling strands of yarn.

As executive editor of a multi-disciplinary journal that publishes the scholarship of teaching and learning, many of my "students" are current professors who write about their teaching experiences. My overall objective, of course, is to find publishable manuscripts. Unfortunately, because most of the submissions are not structured in a way that can report the cause of the author's results, they are returned without being sent to reviewers and my teaching takes the form of a rejection letter. One lesson is predominant and that comes from Richard Light, et al. in By Design: "You cannot save by analysis what you bungled by design." The typical rejection letter reads "in order to be of use to our readers, we would need to know why you undertook this project. What did you see in your students that you wanted to change or improve? What did others do when confronted by a similar situation? Why did you decide on the intervention you used? What learning objectives would your students do better through this change in your teaching?" The problem with the submissions is not that the work the instructor did was not good or useful; rather the problem is that the work probably was good and cannot be published because it did not begin anywhere. Without a beginning, without a clear description of how the instructor's students were doing in meeting the course learning objectives before the intervention, there cannot be a comparison with their work after the intervention to determine whether there was any change, or if the change was due to the intervention.

Unwinding an instructor's "tangled yarn" begins with the need for making explicit course learning objectives that are as clear, observable, and measurable as possible. It is amazing how many professors teach without defining their course goals in student learning terms. The first question is: "What will students know and or be able to do when they complete the course?" Without that beginning there is no way to find out whether or not any teaching has been successful at creating learning.

My classroom teaching consists of providing background and skills to graduate students interested in academic careers. I teach five courses and a practicum each year to create scaffolding for future faculty members to be able to accomplish their professional teaching objectives. Where do we begin? With learning objectives, of course. It is amazing to my students that so few (almost none) of their professors ever have provided them with clear objectives, let alone rubrics for understanding the qualities of outstanding work. The ease with which courses can be designed and taught with clear learning objectives "unwinds" the difficulties both new and experienced teachers face. Those students who have taught previously find themselves revitalized by the scholarly approach to teaching and learning. Future instructors find confidence that they will be able to communicate their disciplinary material to newcomers to their fields (their students). They all find that intellectual engagement with the teaching and learning process make it more stimulating and interesting than the "fly by the seat of your pants" approach.

I teach future and current faculty to make their lives as instructors safer. By helping them design their courses to be clear about goals, smart about assignments, and overall to meet the needs of their students' learning, I help prevent uncomfortable and dangerous situations where students complain (rightfully) that they were not informed of what the purpose of the course was, what the course assignments were to accomplish, and how the instructor (and they) would know when their work met the criteria for excellence.

As I said, I am driven by my dislike of ignorance when knowledge is available to help people succeed. As a teacher I try to provide the essential information to my students (both current and future faculty) so that they can accomplish their goals and help their students learn. I want to prevent the disastrous mismatch of my own student experience.

* * * * *

Laurie Richlin is Director of the Claremont Graduate University Preparing Future Faculty Program, Director of the regional Lilly Conferences on College and University Teaching, Executive Editor of the *Journal of Excellence in College Teaching* and President of the International Alliance of Teacher Scholars. She received her doctorate on higher education from the Claremont University and her dissertation research on alternate faculty scholarship and received the national Gratzke award from the American Association of University Administrators. Recent publications include articles in *The Scholarship of Teaching Educating Professional, New Directions in Teaching and Learning* a chapter in *Successful Faculty Development Strategies* and a coauthored book *Improving a College/University Teaching Evaluation System*. She has taught Journalism, Career Development, and writing and research methods. Richlin developed and implemented the Teaching Assistant Development Program at the University of California, was Educator in Residence at colleges in Kentucky and Indiana and under an FIPSE grant served as Director of the Office of Faculty Development at the University of Pittsburg before returning to California.

Chapter 10

Thar's Gold in Them Thar Souls

By Louis Schmier

I remember the events as though they just happened. The date is January 6, 1995. The time is 9:15 a.m. The place is room 140 in West Hall on the campus of Valdosta State College in South Georgia. It is the first day of the winter quarter session of my first year American history survey class. I had grouped the students into clusters of five to engage in a biographical interview exercise with which I was experimenting for the first time. The interview was to be the first step of a week-long process of breaking the barriers that separated the students, building bridges among them, and forging a classroom community. Believing that the process included shattering the wall that often existed between me, the professor, and them, the students, I had to be a part of the class rather than stand apart from it.

As the interviews began, I sat down with one cluster and began interviewing and being interviewed. This group of students decided to pair off. I was paired with a young lady named Kim. You have to know some important facts about Kim. She was eighteen years old, African-American, the first in her entire extended family to graduate high school, much less go to college, and she was in the college's "developmental studies" program. In those days, "developmental studies" was a nice way, a jargon way, a politically correct way, of saying "remedial." At that time, "developmental studies" meant that no one truly had confidence that students like Kim were of college material, that we were bowing to the political pressures that demanded every student have access to a college education, that while we offered students access, we really didn't take any responsibility for their success, that we didn't really believe they belonged, that we'd go through the motions of overcoming their deficiencies by putting them into a remedial math or English course while we threw them into other regular classes, that we'd take their checks for a year, that we would then suspend them, and that we'd then blame them for their failure to take advantage of our self-proclaimed "Herculean effort."

So there I was with Kim, as we asked each other unusual, conversation-provoking questions:

I asked her, "If you were a plant, which one would you say you are and why?"

"A weed because I can't never be a pretty flower to nobody," she bashfully answered.

I asked her, "If you were a material, what would you say you are and why?"

"Rough sandpaper, real rough, because I always rub people the wrong way," she shot back.

I asked her, "What's your most memorable childhood experience?"

"Ain't got none," she sighed.

With my antennae on full power, I asked her, "What is your biggest regret?"

And she sadly and slowly answered, "Bein' a mistake."

With each heavy answer to these light questions, my antennae shot up higher and higher, and my radar went on increased alert. Then, we came to what we both later would call THE QUESTION.

I asked her, "What is something you would like to stop doing?"

Kim hesitated. Then, in a near whisper, she leaned over and said, "I'd like to stop drinking."

This time I struck up a conversation, "Why do you drink?"

"To have friends . . . and to get rid of the stress. But, I'm no alcoholic. It just started in high school."

"How long you been doing it?"

"About three years. Started in when I was in ninth grade. No one knew because no one in my family cottons to drinkin', but no one would really have cared if they know'd no how."

"Will you take a drink today?"

"Already did. I'm stressin' about being here in college. I'm the first one in my family. Everyone is supposedly so proud of me and expectin' so much of me. First time anyone has really noticed me. I can't let anyone down."

"Going to take any more drinks?"

"Probably."

"Well, don't," I said, not knowing at the time I was doing an Al-anon approach with a tone that I didn't at the time realize was smart alecky. "Don't take another drink today. Don't worry about yesterday; don't think about tomorrow; just think about today. Tomorrow, when you come to class, I'll quietly ask you if you're clean. Just take it one day at a time."

She looked at me. Her surprised stare was quickly followed by a giggle as you giggle when you feel a combination of fear, hope, and embarrassment. Then, it came her turn to ask me the same question.

"Dr. Schmier, what is something you would like to stop doing?"

Without thinking, for no reason I can offer to this day—sometimes you just don't ask a why—I blurted out, "I'd like to stop biting my nails!" As soon as I heard myself saying those words, I wanted to lunge forward and grab them before they entered Kim's ears.

"Let me see them," she asked.

Nervously, I stretched out my hands, palms down, fingers stiffly spread apart. Now to what I was saying. You have to understand that, unlike Kim, I was an addict. I was a ferocious nail biter. I was a "nailaholic." I was like a hyena gnawing on a dead carcass! And when the nails were gone, I went after the cuticles. My fingers looked like a war zone, so ravaged they would have qualified for Marshall Plan aid. Without exaggeration, I couldn't remember a day in my life of fifty-five years that I hadn't bitten my nails. A day never had passed that I could remember when one or usually more of my fingers wasn't hurting, bleeding, or infected.

"Why do you bite your nails?" Kim asked.

"I don't know, but there must be a reason. Just a bad habit, I guess," I sheepishly answered.

"You gonna bite your nails some more today?"

"Probably. Sure."

"Well," Kim went on with a seriousness I didn't really hear. "Why don't you just not do it. Don't worry about all them years before you bit your nails and don't think about that you'll bite them tomorrow. Just don't bite your nails today. And tomorrow, when we come to class, I'll ask you if you're clean. Just take it one day at a time."

I put one hand to my face, squeezed my cheeks together and covered my mouth so I wouldn't utter the not-so-nice thoughts about Kim and her proposal that flashed through my mind. Now it was my turn to giggle as you giggle when you feel a combination of fear and embarrassment.

I thought at that moment that neither one of us thought much of our mutual challenge or offer of assistance. I thought neither one of us thought the other was serious. I knew I didn't. As was my practice, after another interviewing question or two, I excused myself and moved on to another cluster.

In those days we had bells to announce the end of the class period. Kim's cluster was by the doorway. I was on the other side of the room in the far corner. My back was to the door. The bell rang. The students jumped up to rush out of the classroom. Kim was among the first to the door. She stopped dead in her tracks, causing a thirty student pile up, turned, and yelled so loud you could have heard her over the din in Atlanta.

"Dr. Schmier! Dr. Schmier!"

I turned. She looked right at me with a desperate seriousness.

"If you stop biting your nails, I'll stop drinking."

Thirty pairs of eyes turned towards me. Damn! Trapped! I could feel the sweat oozing from my palms. My lips tightened. My abdominal muscles went into a sudden spasm. My legs went numb. A wave of nausea crashed over me. It was one of those "put your money where your mouth is" times. I answered a quieter and nervous, "Okay."

Kim smiled. No, she beamed. Her eyes lit up. "Good, we're clean for the rest of the day and then some." With that affirmation, she turned and rushed out the door.

That night I learned what withdrawal is. I had the delirium tremors. There were stubble marks on the bathroom walls. They would have been claw marks if I had nails. I took so many cold showers, I looked like a bleached prune. I had not so nice thoughts of Kim. I dug my finger stubbles deep into my cold, sweaty palms. I bit my lower lip until I almost drew blood. I grimaced with achy desires to nibble at the stubble. How many packs of gum I went through, I don't know. I paced. I cursed Kim. I went to the computer to distract myself, but I was up and down like the proverbial yo-yo. I drank gallons of water. I went to bed wearing gloves. I tossed and turned and sweated. I had not so nice thoughts of

Kim. I only hoped she was having the same agonies. It would be sweet revenge and justice, I thought to myself. Through the entire night my angelic Susan lovingly held me, talked with me, stayed up and played backgammon with me. I got through the night—barely.

The next morning, Kim walked into class with a "You clean, Dr. Schmier?"

"I had a sleepless night, but I'm clean," I proudly answered through my tired fog. "You clean?"

"Sure 'nuf. I didn't sleep much either," Kim replied with equal pride.

Both Kim and I went cold turkey that day. For six weeks, day after day after day, we asked each other at the beginning of the class, "You clean?" For six weeks, day after day after day, we each answered with an increasing sense of accomplishment, "Yep." For six weeks, day after day after day, we exchanged stories of our agonies, challenges, near slip-ups, our need to support each other. Sometimes I called Kim; sometimes she called me. Heck, I couldn't cheat even if I wanted. The entire class knew. Kim had spies everywhere. Students in other classes somehow found out and they'd ask if I was clean as I walked the hall or entered the classroom. I couldn't walk campus without hearing a "You clean, Dr. Schmier?" coming from somewhere uttered by a strange voice. I'd be munching on a sinful doughnut in the Student Union and a student, someone whom I had never seen, would pass me with a warning, "Only the doughnut, Dr. Schmier, not the nails." I'd be in a store or walking in the mall and someone would come up to me with a warning, "Don't cheat on Kim."

Heard of the Flying Nun? Well, at times I was almost the "Flying Professor." My nails were so thin they'd flap in the wind like wings and nearly lift me off the ground. Not being accustomed to any length or to hanging in free space, they'd droop over the tips of my fingers. They were as strong as wet tissue paper. They'd break, crack, tear, or crumble under the slightest pressure. They were always ragged. There were so many emery boards sticking out from my pants, shirt, and coat pockets, I looked like a porcupine. The temptation to sin, to nibble, to break my promise to Kim was always there. But, the constant image of Kim with her struggle not to secret a nip meant I had to take an emery board to the ever-ragged nails rather than my incisors.

After six weeks of being cold-turkey clean, after six weeks of agony, I decided to give myself a present. I went to my wife's manicurist. Christa took one look at my war-torn, scarred fingers, and nearly fainted. Out came the heavy duty stuff. The Himalayas were nothing compared to height and hardness of the granite-hard scar tissue. As she worked on my cuticle scar tissue, she commented that she felt like she was carving a marble statue. With every sweep of her file on my nails, she said it was like working with wet tissue paper. After about an hour and a half, she surrendered and said, "That's all I can do for now. It'll take six months to get your nails decent."

Then an impish impulse overcame me. "Paint my right pinky with that 'whore red' polish."

"Why?"

"I have my reasons."

"I know why," Christa slyly smiled. "Susan told me yesterday you guys argued about you wanting a tattoo and she not letting you get one. Now you're getting even."

I smiled back. She was right. That previous evening, Susan and I had an interesting discussion. I was so proud of having stopped biting my nails, I was strutting my feathers. I told Susan I now wanted a tattoo. Susan told me in no uncertain terms I could not get a tattoo.

"You women talk about having control of you body," I angrily asserted with finality. "What about us men? What are you going to do if I come home tomorrow with a tattoo?"

Susan smiled. Quietly she said in a loving voice of finality, "Honey, it's not what I'm going to do; it's what I'm not going to do."

End of discussion. Defeated! The nail polish on my pinky nail was my revenge. At the same time, it was for me a sign of my accomplishment. That night, looking at my manicure, I felt so proud of myself. Then, just before I hit the bed I heard a devilish voice in my ear.

"Why don't you celebrate, Louis. You deserve it. What will one little nibble do? No one will know. You really deserve a reward for all that you've gone through. It won't hurt."

I resisted that tempting voice for about an hour. Then, I surrendered to that satanic whisper. I raised my right hand to my mouth.

Now, before I go farther in this story let me stop so you'll understand what was about to happen. I am totally right-brained. I am totally left-handed. I would gladly give you my right hand. If I did, contrary to biblical implication, I wouldn't be making any great sacrifice. I'd never miss it. I always, I always, always, always bit the nails on my left hand first and then went on to gnaw on my right. This time, however, for whatever mysterious reason—I don't ask—I unconsciously broke a half century habit and I went to my right hand first. Just as I was about to sin, I saw that pinky painted in that "whore red" color, thought of Kim, thought of how I would feel betrayed if she was doing the same sort of celebration. I hesitated. I felt like I was about to be a whore as I stared at the "whore red." And, I slowly put my hand down. That night was the kind of hellish night I thought I had put behind me. It was a night of cold showers, gloves, sweat, nails digging into my palms, gallons of water, tossing and turning, backgammon, and consoling.

The next day, Kim came into class, grabbed my hands, looked and said, "Dr. Schmier, you. . . ." She interrupted herself, leaned over—almost putting her nose to my pinky—and quickly asked in amazement, "What's that shit on your nail?"

I told her the story. Her eyes filled with tears. "You need me, don't you."

"I guess I do. We need each other to do this."

"Nobody has ever needed me before."

The next day, Kim came to class with her pinky nail painted. And so it went until the end of the term. As my nail grew, Kim's confidence grew. She slowly became a leader in her "triad." She slowly came out from her remedial shadows. She slowly silenced her silence. She slowly dared to go to the heart of her heart. A faint glow appeared and slowly brightened. She increasingly smiled. A few of the students appeared in class with painted pinkies, asking Kim and me to help them break their "bad" habits.

On the last day of every class, we do closure. It is the day each of us, me included, reflect and share on where each of us has been, how far we've come, and, hopefully, where we're going. We share what the class meant and what we are taking from it. I brought in an emery board and after all the students had shown their objects was going to talk about what this class meant to me. One student stood up, showed us an empty snuff container and told us how Kim had helped him start breaking his habit. Another student brought in a cigarette pack and told us how she had helped him cut down on his smoking. And so it went around the classroom. As it turned out, the last student to stand up was Kim. She arose, tears streaming down her cheeks, and silently held up an empty shot glass in one hand and a bottle of nail polish in the other. The class went wild. Others held up their painted pinkies. There wasn't a dry eye in the room. We all applauded, cheered, and hugged. I never did talk about the emery board. Kim had said it all. Unnoticed, I put the emery board back in my pocket and the class came to an end.

On April 6, three months to the day since I last had my fingers in my mouth, I found a simple handwritten letter lying matter-of-factly—almost camouflaged—amidst the cluttered landfill of my desk. I almost didn't notice it. That would have been tragic. I picked it up nonchalantly and started reading it. With every passing word, I realized that this was a letter not to be read casually. It was from Kim. I slowed down. I stopped halfway through, took a deep breath, wiped away a tear or two, unwrapped a Tootsie Pop, and finished reading, grabbing at every word through the haze of my glassy eyes.

Dr. Schmier:

I am really glad that I made a promise to myself and to you to stop drinking because of the fact that it was really bad for my spirit and my health. I guess I just needed someone to care enough to get me to see what I wanted to see, but didn't have the courage to see. No one in my immediate family drinks. So it was not anything I picked up at home. I drank while in high school. That is when it started. Hanging around my friends and watching them drink made me want to do it. Well, now I know no one made me do anything. I did it all to myself. I just didn't want to be left out of things and was afraid of being thought of as a jerk. I guess I just didn't have the confidence and strength to take the chance of saying no. I wasn't happy about it, but I didn't think I could do anything about it until you came along.

I made the promise at first just to impress you, but when you proudly showed me your nails after your first manicure and bragged to everyone in the class that the dark purple nail polish on your pinky was a sign of our deal, I knew that you weren't bulling me but you were showing everyone who you really are. So, I had to do the same. I also saw that pinky as a sign that you needed me as much as I needed you. That feeling of being needed and being something made me feel that I was important and could do something for others. It made me feel good. That's when I started doing it for myself. Since my promise, I feel renewed and like a better person because I have been clean since the start of the quarter and because I have cleaned my spirit and attitude and body. I'm happier and more honest. I like being myself and being able to turn down drinks. I feel like people respect me more now that I have stopped drinking. I respect myself more. That's more important, I think. I have found out that I can handle my problems without the use of a drink and that I don't need a drink to solve my problems, which it doesn't anyway. I like that. I used to only drink when something was deeply on my mind or I was depressed. I now have found out because of our deal that there are other ways to have a good time.

I feel really GOOD knowing that I have many people, especially you and the others in the class, backing me and believing in me. But what really makes me feel best is that I believe in myself now. I believe now that there's a lump of gold inside me to mine. It makes me wonder that if I have it in me to put a lid on the bottle, what lids I can open in myself. I believe that if I can deal with drinking there isn't anything I can't do here in school and everywhere else. Thanks for caring and believing in me and asking me each day if I was clean.

Please keep your pinky painted to remind you and show others that you will always be there to help someone start becoming who they can be just like you did with me. You clean today? Happy anniversary.

I saw Kim a few days a week during the spring quarter. We'd always greet each other with a "You clean?" And, we'd both answer with a proud, "Yes!" Contrary to expectations, Kim "hung around" the college after that term. We saw less and less of each other as the terms passed. She left the remedial program, became an education major, and graduated with a high GPA. I like to think I had something to do with that.

Since that quarter, my pinky is always painted. I change the color every week or so. It has become a symbol of "my story," a "genesis story." It has become more than a bond between Kim and me. It has become a symbol of my commitment to be that person who is there to help each student help himself/herself to become the person he or she is capable of becoming.

Students always ask me about that pinky during our "what do you want to know about me" beginning-of-the-semester session. They are always touched. I read them Kim's letter, a copy of which I always carry with me in my wallet. Some get teary-eyed. So do I.

This story has miraculous powers for the host of Kims who are "out there." That fact was driven home for me two years later in the fall of 1997. I was on the campus of a flagship institution offering a series of addresses and workshops. One of the sessions was a conversation with a couple of hundred honor students in a vast hall. We talked, discussed, argued over my philosophy of education and my teaching methods. I jumped off the stage, moving all over the place so that I could be up close to almost all of them. We went at each other for about an hour. I was running late for a faculty workshop. A Dean, who was shepherding me, yelled a "time to go" and our exchange came to an abrupt end. As I was walking up the aisle, nearly at the back of the hall, I noticed out of the corner of my eye a questioning hand waving in the front.

"One more question," I yelled out as I stopped, turned, ran back down the aisle and across the front row.

"We have no time," the Dean yelled back with a smile.

"It's my session," I yelled back to the delight of the students.

It proved to be one of those "you don't ask" moments. I looked at the student, thinking that she was going to throw one more disagreeing question at me about grades as lousy indicators of ability, learning, and potential. Instead, she asked, "Why is your nail painted?"

After a moment's hesitation, I told her and all the students, but especially her, the story of me and Kim, and read aloud, with cracking and hesitating voice, Kim's letter.

"Time to go home," I loudly whispered. As I walked up the far aisle, a bunch of students followed me. A crowd gathered around me at the back of the hall, haranguing me about my philosophy of education and non-lecturing, non-testing, engaged project teaching methods. I hadn't noticed that the young lady who had asked about the nail had followed me. As I was about to be rushed out of the hall, she tapped me on the shoulder. Something told me to tell the Dean to wait a minute. I turned towards her.

"That story really got to me. You know I'm an honors student here. But, I'm like Kim. I haven't been sober one day since I came here. There's a lot of pressure on me. My parents expect nothing but A's and I drink to get away from it all. My grades are going to hell, and my boyfriend says if I don't drink with him at the parties, he'll leave me. I'm afraid of being alone up here and I'm afraid of what might happen when I get drunk. It almost did last night. I have no one to help me. I want to stop drinking. No one around here cares if I stand tall or lie on my back. Can I be another Kim for you? Will you e-mail each day and ask me if I'm clean?"

I just stood there, motionless. The Dean just stood there, motionless. "I won't be back on campus for a day or two, but I'll e-mail you. Just start being clean today."

"Okay!" And, she ran off.

Three days later, I e-mailed Judy (not her real name) a simple "You clean today."

She immediately replied with a message that I printed out and is pinned on the wall of what I call my "sacred objects of teaching":

> I was so happy to get your e-mail. I didn't really think I'd get one. I was afraid you weren't for real. I just was hoping against hope you weren't a high paid bullshitter like everyone else. Yeah, I'm clean. Have been for two days. Feels good. Already had lots of fights with my so-called boyfriend. There's a big party on campus this weekend. I was going to go home instead of going. Running away. Afraid I couldn't stay clean. My boyfriend is pissed because he wants to drink and get me into bed and screw me blind. But, now I have the strength to go to that party and not drink. I can say no to him because I don't feel alone now, and I don't care what he or anyone says. Please ask if I'm clean every day. You clean, Dr. Schmier?

I e-mailed her every day for six months. She talked; I listened. She sobered up. Went cold turkey. Turned her performance around. Dumped her boyfriend. And she discovered in the process that, though she was labeled an honors student because of her grades, she slowly could call herself an honors person because of the person she saw that she now was. I'll just say that we e-mail each other occasionally. It's what Judy calls "a maintenance check-up."

You know, Kim is right. The rich vein of human potential is never absent in anyone. It's there, hidden deep, hidden sometimes under an uninviting surface, waiting to be brought up into the light of day. Teaching, then, is the mining for gold, and we teachers are the prospectors whose task is to invite students to dig along side us as their own prospectors mining for their own pay dirt.

Imagine if we were all willing to go at a group of students, or just one student, the way a prospector goes at a mountainside with a pick and shovel; if we believed that everything will go our way regardless of what happens; if we didn't take a discouraging "no" to our dreams; if we weren't deterred by the unassuming barrenness of the terrain because we knew that deep within the rock of the students' being lay an untold rich abundance of glittering potential.

I have discovered that if we help students mine themselves, expecting to find a vein of gold, we almost always will. Getting to that rich ore, however, isn't something that is easy. It takes sweat and effort and endurance. Progress can be slow. The way through the rock can be rocky. Sometimes you have to feel your way in the darkness; sometimes you have to delicately pick; sometimes you have to shovel; sometimes you have to blast. The rubble has to be hauled out. The tunnel has to be shored up. There are going to be the inevitable cave-ins. You'll battle your aching body and your strained emotions as well as the rock. At times, you'll feel as if you can't go on. Nothing is guaranteed. Sometimes you'll take a wrong first turn or your tools will break or you'll face impenetrable hard rock or you won't be able to dig deep enough with the tools you've got.

But, if and when you get down to the bedrock of a student's human potential, you will strike it rich. And I have discovered that once a student is aware of the pay dirt of talent inside himself/herself, once a student is in touch with the wealth of the particular individuality of his or her own genius, once a student sees the brilliance of his or her selfhood, and once a student starts mining the treasure of his or her own unique potential, the vein seldom peters out. And there are few places on earth outside the classroom where this kind of opportunity can present itself.

* * * * *

His name is Louis Schmier. He received his Ph.D. from the University of North Carolina. Since 1991, he stopped historical research and has devoted all his time and energy to the classroom, and has made students his profession. His concern is more on the learning of students than his teaching, more concerned with students as human beings than with subject. In 1993, he began a series of electronic sharing of his beliefs about the nature and purpose of an education, a commemoration of student learning and achievement, a proclamation of faith in students and a celebration of teaching. These thoughts have been published in two volumes. In short, he is more concerned with reaching for students than reaching the height of professional reputation. And he finds that the satisfaction of touching one student is far more satisfying and fulfilling than the publication of any book or the presentation at any conference. He holds the rank of Professor of History at Valdosta State University.

Chapter 11

Identity and Integrity of a Teacher

By Bruce Saulnier

When someone at a conference asks me. "What do you teach?" why is my answer always, "students"? Why, year after year, do I attend conferences on teaching and learning when my field of study is Computer Information Systems? Why is my scholarship in what the late Ernest Boyer termed "the scholarship of teaching" rather than in the discipline of "computer information systems"?

Noted educator Parker Palmer has become one of my spiritual guides as I venture along the path of life. He postulates that "Good teaching cannot be reduced to mere technique; good teaching comes from the identity and integrity of the teacher." But what is my identity and my integrity? And how can I bring my identity and integrity into my relationships with students?

I've long since stopped pretending that I have answers to such questions. On a good day I might be considering a proper question. If the truth be known, on some days I haven't a clue as to what is going to happen in my classes. And, if the truth also be known, somewhere deep inside (in a place where I still fear to go) is a little voice that wants to tell me that you will not accept me if you knew that I really do not have a clue. But I'll take that risk, and lay before you some of my guiding principles in the hopes that they may provide you with a brief window into my soul:

I believe that I have a genuine calling to be a teacher. It is a role consistent with who I am. There are some aspects of being a professor that I find quite difficult, and others (such as teaching) in which I thrive.

I try to be the type of teacher I would want my own children to have. Every student is somebody' s child and a person of worth, and it is both an honor and a sacred trust to be placed before them.

I try to remember what it felt like to be a student—the uncertainty, the curiosity, the self-doubt, and all of the other emotions of self-discovery initially encountered by 18-25 year-olds, emotions with which we as adults sometimes have great difficulty.

I believe that I am not a teacher, but a fellow learner—more of a mentor in the learning process rather than a sage on a stage. I have much more to learn as I travel along the way, and students have much to teach me provided that I am willing to remain teachable.

I believe in the principles of learner-centered teaching. I do not teach my discipline; rather, I use my discipline to teach students.

Any glimpse into my reality and who I bring into the classroom would be incomplete if I did not conclude by giving thanks for a few of my blessings:

For coming from being the first in my family to attend college to being a college professor;

For my working class background, which taught me not only the value of hard work, but to honor each and every human being as a person of worth;

For my father, for modeling appropriate behavior, for students and children indeed learn what they see more than what they hear;

For the faculty of Defiance College, particularly Dr. John Luchies, who took a raw, working-class kid with great self-doubt and transformed him into a student who believed in himself and his potential;

For working in a place such as Quinnipiac University which, over the years, has allowed me to truly be who I am and to walk the path that is right for me;

For my students, who are my true calling and make it a joy to not come to work, but come to play, on a daily basis;

For my fellow employees over the years—Larry Harris who took a chance and offered a faculty position to a 25 year old kid still "wet behind the years"; fellow department faculty Ed Moody, Vince Celeste, and Della Lee-Lien with whom I have worked and played for a combined total of 85 years; Provost Harry Bennett who taught me that patience is indeed one of life's greatest virtues in solving problems; "coach" Larry Levine who told me in his congratulatory e-mail that he was thinking of "letting me start" a couple of games; and others simply too numerous to mention;

For my immediate family—my children Kyle and Melanie who now approach adulthood and whom I love dearly, and my wife Janice who after close to 30 years of marriage is still my soul mate and my best friend;

For my extended family—Brad, Jeff, Jim, Dick, John, and countless others—without whom I would have many times lost my way;

For St. Francis of Assisi, whose prayer that begins, "Lord, make me an instrument of Thy peace" serves as a daily reminder of what matters in this life; and

For my Creator, for the talents I have received and the path I am privileged to walk.

* * * * * *

Bruce Saulnier is Professor of Computer Information Systems at Quinnipiac University in Hamden, Connecticut. He has been active in the Scholarship of Teaching and Learning for a number of years with numerous papers delivered at the annual conferences of the International Society for Exploring Teaching and Learning, Lilly Conferences on College and University teaching, International Conference on College Teaching and Learning, and Information Systems Education Conference. Current research interests include Teaching and Learning Spiritual Activities, Learner Centered Teaching in Cyberspace, and Building Community in the Online Classroom. Bruce is a past recipient of the Quinnipiac University Faculty Member of the Year Award, was named the 2002 Connecticut Professor of the Year by the Carnegie Foundation for the Advancement of Teaching, and is Past-President and a Distinguished Fellow of the International Society for Exploring Teaching and Learning.

Chapter 12

Teaching as Leadership, Love, and Forgiveness—From the Points of View of Tragedy, Comedy, and Chaos

BY DR. BARBARA MOSSBERG

Educe [l. *educere* to draw out, lead forth, fr. *e* + *educere* to lead) 1. to bring out (as something latent) **syn** educe, evoke, elicit, extract, extort, to draw out something hidden, latent, or reserved. EDUCE implies the bringing out of something potential or latent < *educed* order out of chaos >

Encyclopedia Brittanica/
Merriam Webster's Collegiate Dictionary 1993

"I am a part of all that I have met"

—from "Ulysses,"
Alfred, Lord Tennyson

"I'm Nobody—who are you?"

—Emily Dickinson

"At last!—to be identified!"

—Emily Dickinson

When I received the distinguished teaching award from the University of Oregon, I was 27 years old, in my second year as an assistant professor of English, wearing a thrift-store long coat with a Roger

Payne Save the Whales button, a floppy felt hat, men's shoes (wider at the toe), knee socks, and my mother's suits from the 40's with shoulder pads (this was before shoulder pads became fashionable and put into store-bought suits, and for all I know, they may be out again). I was insecure as a professor, but in looking back at myself then, I am amazed how unself-consciously I went about my business as The Professorate. If my dress was in any way out of the norm of this august body, it certainly never entered my mind. I was too absorbed with the responsibility of serving as a teacher. It was my worry about doing right by my students that occupied my waking moments. Many of my students were older than I. Many were not sure that English literature was useful or mattered. I had no idea if I belonged in the academy. Sure, I had been hired, but I thought this was a lucky mistake and that it would be discovered as such sooner or later. The challenge that grounded my energies centered around the fact that, after all, to the students, I *was* a professor. They didn't know better. I could not let them down.

I would be in my office till 11 p.m., then up at 5 a.m. even on Sundays. I was trying to figure out strategies that would engage my students so that they learned what *they felt* was vital to them and what *they thought* they needed to know, not only in the long run, for careers and life changes and crises, but right now.

In this I faced some practical obstacles that had to be overcome if students were to feel that what was being learned was essential to their being. For one, it was very early in the morning to be learning, and our topic was Tragedy. Euripides, Sophocles, Shakespeare, Strindberg, O'Neill—this was pretty heavy for 8:30 a.m. And I knew I was competing for students' attention with the need for new shoes, the lack of a Saturday night date, parents going through divorce, the football season, two jobs, a skateboard injury, a parent questioning their major, a possible pregnancy, and any number of other things which were occupying their minds. Even so, I would go into every class excited. I had been engaging with the material: *what is important about this?* And that was wonderful. I was also half dead from worrying: *how will this go?* I suffered enormous doubts and dread. But I was mostly curious to see what would happen. There was alchemy between these minds and those texts chronicling someone's efforts to make sense of our lives and crises and opportunities and consciousness. The more I planned and prepared for such encounters across minds and cultures and generations, the more I realized that you could never predict just where a question you asked or they asked would lead. You would be out there off script, discovering what you know that you didn't even know you knew, what was possible to learn with and from each other. And I would become elated. I would be jumping up and down in my excitement about what was happening to each person, to all of us together.

"We had the experience, but missed the meaning."
—T.S. Eliot, *The Four Quartets*

My goal was to make sure that on any day, my students knew that their presence in the class was vital to what was learned—that learning could not happen without their participation and contribution. Since their own knowledge of the material and self-knowledge were evolving in the process, I could not predict what experiences and sensibility would be brought to our learning activities and how each student's contributions would spark another's or add up. I could plan and prepare this chemistry of ideas, but the interpretation of the resulting mixture, and how that would combine and be added to, I could not know. I was setting off a "chaotic reaction" of events designed to involve each student in vital and transforming ways. What questions would invoke what they felt they knew something about? What could *draw out* the meaning of the stories we were reading? What ways of working together would our students experience as valuable? How could we make the course meaningful to their lives?

In the beginning I would be asked, *Why do you teach the way you do.* As a young professor I pondered what was meant by this (and its implications for tenure, certainly). What behaviors generate this question (or is everyone asked this)? What was different, and was this a good thing or a bad thing? If I did not teach the way I had been taught, that was probably because I had been taught by professors, and as a student I could not presume that I would or could or should be that assured man in the tweed coat, smoking a pipe. My only claim to being in the academy was that I loved reading and thinking about it and getting people excited and inspired by it. If I felt it was a fluke that I was a professor, somehow that knowledge freed me up. I could engage with the material and my students as myself. I am temperamentally more a coach, a drama director, a camp counselor leading songs around the campfire. I am both a clown and far too earnest to be good company. I always have felt that my students probably know me better than anyone else in my life, including my family, because in most daily interactions we do not struggle to explore and express our deepest ideas and vulnerabilities as we do when we are teaching.

Winning the teaching award and other teaching recognition from students and peers at the university and nationally gave me an encouraging feeling of at least belonging. But if in one way I did not presume I belonged in the profession I am so in love with, it was my professors and colleagues who brought out or "drew forth" whatever was in me that led to my life as a teacher. It has now been almost 30 years that I have been teaching, along with serving in academic leadership roles in support of teaching and learning. As I reflect on what for me is the joy of teaching, I begin with a story that frames my purpose as an educator. It is one of gratitude.

Story, 1968-1969

I am a student at UCLA, and my courses are large lecture classes of hundreds of students each, some so large that all of us in the class don't fit in the auditorium and some have to sit in satellite rooms watching TV screens of the professor. I have largely sympathetic and charismatic and wry TA's who lead discussions, but no interaction with any professors, and if I am absent, I know it makes no difference. One spring week, I take off for Stanford and Berkeley to visit friends. It is the third week of the term, and I am enrolled in an English 2 class required to graduate. A paper had been assigned. I had not had to do a paper up until that point in my other enormous introductory courses. I turned in something I hoped was "a paper," and then I headed up Highway 101 north. A week later, I returned to campus and called my professor, Randy Helms. "Hello," I said, "this is Barbara Ann Clarke, I am in your Monday-Wednesday-Friday class at 10:30, Section 223—." He broke in, "Barbara, where have you been? I have missed you, and the class has missed you. You wrote an interesting paper. Come see me." Twenty minutes later, I was in his office, barefoot, since I did not even take the time to put on shoes (this was the late sixties, and the cast of *Hair* would come on campus in the afternoons, and there were always protests going on, so my bare feet were probably not even noticed).

The idea that I had a role to play in our class, and, in fact, a responsibility to be there, was shocking. It was also transforming. With one stroke, a professor made me part of a learning community and activated a voice, a conscience, a desire to contribute, a sense that I had something to contribute. This was "educing," the bringing out of potential that is the root of our word for "education." I became an English major, and made the decision to dedicate my life to working to promote environments for learning in which students feel essential to the process. Ever since, whether I've had a class of 40 or 200 or 500 (and I have had even larger), I have worked to instill a sense of each student's inextricable role in our learning.

Story, 1978

19th century American Literature, University of Oregon. I'm a professor, and today, we are studying Ralph Waldo Emerson's "Self Reliance." To the class of 300, I say, "You are a Salvation Army worker, it's Christmas, and you ask Emerson for a donation. What does he say? OK, everyone: write down what you think." I then walk through the aisles, asking people to read what they wrote. What did you base that on, I ask. They read from a passage. But the next person disagrees. The next person has a different idea altogether. How can this be? I ask, why is it that we each read the same words in the same order, and that *you* said this, and *you* said that, and *you* said something else? I ask another student, What do *you* make of this? We discuss the variety of responses and the students create a "theory" for what accounts for the difference in our readings and conclusions about Emerson's philanthropic soul. I stand at the side, then at the back row. Like wind in the grass, my moving through the room creates a stir: newspapers are hurriedly folded, people sit up. There is No Safe Place. You will be asked to contribute no matter where you sit. And what is worse, missing class will not get you off the hook. It's not even possible to pass if you don't come. Why not? I ask people to get up and role play: you are Emerson, and you are the Salvation Army worker asking him for a contribution. You are his kid, asking why he gave (or did not give) the donation. The student playing Emerson gets a consulting team to give him advice. Having learned that students would stop taking notes when I stop talking and their peers begin, I give tests and quizzes that include what was said in the discussion. I make getting a good grade dependent upon the students' respect and value of each other's contributions. Then we explore our understandings that reflect the class as a whole. We put on dramas of the material and stage debates and trials (Oedipus as a mass murderer, for example). I ask every person to keep a journal on how their thinking about the course affects their lives, and I also require people to submit questions every week. I review these and answer them both collectively and individually. I want what I do as a professor, in my lecturing, testing, and grading, to show how much I value what the students think and say, and what matters to them. Students can see themselves in what is taught, and what is tested. In these various ways, I tried to carry forth the lesson I had learned from my UCLA professor Randy Helms about how to have the student feel essential to the learning process. I tried to make concrete the understanding of how much would be missed without each person's contribution.

This goal translated to my work as an academic administrator. I have sought positions where the stated and lived ethos is the value of being "student-centered" and "learning centered." I am sure that my English professor took for granted his own work to bring a student back to the flock; most of our faculty does this all in a day's work. Yet the impact on student learning that acknowledging and recognizing what someone has to offer seems to be deeply connected with leadership (" e + *ducere* to lead"). At the University of Oregon, as a faculty member, I was asked by Robert Berdahi, Richard Hersh, and other academic leaders to speak for a few minutes at a program on behalf of the University to the State System of Higher Education Board on the humanities. Were they useful? Were they practical in an age increasingly concerned with fiscal realities and driven by new technologies? I felt a keen sense of responsibility in this task to articulate the value of humanities at a time of increasing technological needs of society and fiscal contingencies. The process led me to reflect on my values. I thought about what matters most in our lives and what is at stake if students do not study the humanities. It was only a fifteen-minute talk, but I do not think I have ever worked so hard to wring out or express whatever I believed. Nor felt such joy—or been so humbly nervous. I was conscious of wanting to do justice to the faith in me to make a good case. The hour before I was to speak, no one could find me. I was holed up in a remote campus bathroom, clutching my stomach. The resulting talk was treated as good news. It was used in various media and became the basis of lectures at the community, state, region, and ultimately, national and international levels. In turn, this representational experience led to my appointments first as a senior Fulbright professor and then as the U.S. Scholar in Residence for the State Department, based in Washington, D.C. In this role I served to articulate the common ground in the values of a diverse, complex American culture and education at the federal and international levels. I then had the chance to serve as Senior Fulbright Distinguished Lecturer, on "Educating for the 21st century: The American Challenge." In turn, this advocacy work on where, how, what, when, and why we should teach, and create, and support environments for discovery and community-building for a profoundly diverse society led to wonderful opportunities. Advocacy was the basis of my affiliation with the American Council on Education as a senior fellow, and to roles serving presidents in exciting institutions committed to innovations in learning, including Hobart and William Smith, National University, and Goddard College, where I served as president. In these roles, my core identity as a teacher invoking the best in what people have to contribute was fundamental to my own ability to nourish a learning community. Currently, I have had the opportunity to help a 21st century California State University pioneer a civic-minded engaged learning community at Ford Ord in the nation's first defense conversion project. Working as a CSU dean I can support work to develop pedagogies and curriculum for learning that incorporate best practices in the context of a global and multicultural vision "the world needs now." I trace the opportunities and honors in these experiences directly to the vision of academic colleagues, in a role identical to a teacher, of what I could contribute to the community.

And this is the point. In all my life, the opportunities I have had to serve have been the function of a vision of someone with an idea of what I could do, or be; and in the effort to rise to the occasion, to do justice to their expectations, one changes and grows. The beholder's eyes develop our Truth and Beauty. We are challenged and inspired to close the gap between our sense of ourselves and what others see or need in us. Our roles and identities, the ways we can serve, are developed as a function of how other people conceive our capacity to contribute. I see leadership as this process: recognizing and developing capacity. At the most fundamental level, is not this what we do as teachers?

It seems to me that we are all dependent for the roles we are to play in life upon the imagination, and generosity of heart and mind, of others who are in a position to let us know the expectations and needs they and society have for us. Whether in a family or organization or academic program, leadership expresses itself as an active commitment and responsibility to recognize and value who we each are, especially in ways we may not be aware of ourselves. The gift of leadership is one of perspective; the vision of "the whole," which connects needs of community with capabilities and commitments of individuals and groups. By definition, we cannot see ourselves this way. We need an outside and global view of what we are and can be. Leadership is the recognition and value of who we are. For each of us to realize our potential, or for that potential to be activated, we need that catalytic vision. In defining leadership as a catalytic process of identifying and evoking in people awareness of their own potential, I think of the image created in humanity's infancy, the story of the Sphinx.

Story, B.C.

According to myth, and later developed by Sophocles in 5th century B.C., cities were like universities. You had to be admitted. Travelers who wanted to enter the city of Thebes needed to pass an entrance test, much like students for today's colleges. This embryonic SAT was developed and administered by an entity commonly held to be a monster, known as "the Sphinx." The Sphinx terrorized the city and its would-be visitors and inhabitants. Her exam had just one question: *what walks on four legs in the morning, two legs at noon,* and *three legs in the afternoon?* Not only were those who could not give the right answer ("man," or as we would say today, "human being") not admitted to the city, they were put to death. Why? This seems like a riddle in itself.

To try to understand the point of this story, couldn't we consider this riddle as a metaphoric understanding of human development? Like the progress of the sun on one day on earth, in the "morning" of our lives as infants we crawl on four legs. Grown up, we walk upright on two (albeit with Advil). In our maturity, the late afternoon of our lives, we walk with the support of a cane (the third "leg"). Thus, the riddle describes human experience of stages in our lives as we age that we all see in each other and experience every day. But as Sophocles tells it, no one could answer the question, and people were dying, until Oedipus came along (and he had his own problems with recognizing reality, but that is another story).

Thus, in this age-old telling, society identifies as a precious and essential community value a life-saving literacy—the ability to answer a riddle. It is fatal not to have the ability to answer riddles, that is, to be unable to see connections between seemingly unrelated concepts. In this case, the riddle requires the integration of different ways reality is expressed in our universe. Change, growth, and development are seen as

one coherent process. If one does not see human development as a con-
tinuity linking where we have been, where we are, and where we are
going, one is not only not fit to live *with;* one is not fit to live at all.

What a harsh and unforgiving judgment for not being able to recognize ourselves in images of the changing human experience. I wonder at
that. But my first question here ponders what is meant in the story by the
fact that up until Oedipus came along, no one could answer this riddle. In
the words of my twelve-year-old daughter, *What is up with that?* How is
it possible to be a human being and not be able to recognize key stages of
our own experience when it is described? What are we to make of the
fact that we cannot see ourselves whole, our experience over time as one
interdependent, interconnected process? I think of the word "revelation,"
which comes from the root Latin word "relevare," which means to lift,
to raise. Perhaps the logic here is that we are able to gain insight with
perspective. Patterns that create meaning are perceived when we have
distance enough. The kind of knowledge required by the society which
developed the Sphinx story can recognize how things that look different—in this case, the formally different stages of human development—
are integrally connected and related. It is relational and contextual knowledge that the community defines as essential for citizenship. At the heart
of this myth and the story Sophocles made of it, we see the mystery in T.
S. Eliot's words, "We had the experience, but missed the meaning."

Perhaps the community suffers when people are unable to recognize
what we all share in our humanity. But who is at fault when the progress
of the sun on one day on earth, in the "morning" of our lives as infants
we crawl on four legs. Grown up, we walk upright on two (albeit with
Advil). In our maturity, the late afternoon of our lives, we walk with the
support of a cane (the third "leg"). Thus, the riddle describes human
experience of stages in our lives as we age that we all see in each other
and experience every day. But as Sophocles tells it, no one could answer
the question, and people were dying, until Oedipus came along (and he
had his own problems with recognizing reality, but that is another story).

Isn't the meaning of this story the role of society's educators and
leaders? Should not the people have been taught this kind of integrative
ability? Or is the meaning we should extract from this that all people who
want to enter a community must have the ability to recognize the charac-
ter and humanity and potential for growth and development in every
person? Here we see a context for the role of leadership and teaching as
one of the ability to recognize, and to help others recognize, growth

potential—what is clear from the "outside" perspective of community. Teachers, as leaders, can provide an encouraging vision of what one has to contribute to society that may be invisible or obscure from the inside out—the way we each live our lives. Relationship seems to be at the heart of revelation. We need each other in order to realize the goodness and value of what we have to offer.

Alert readers will remember that the title of this article is "Leadership, Love, and Forgiveness," and may wonder what love has to do with it, much less forgiveness, as part of understanding teaching as revelation and visionary leadership. My thought, in giving this essay such a title, comes from my recent rereading of the poem "Ulysses," by Alfred, Lord Tennyson, written in 1833. Permit me, then, to take another story from the humanities to express my understanding of what to me is at the heart of the joy of teaching. In this poem, Tennyson has a narrator who is a leader, reflecting upon a life of adventurous governance which is not yet over, but is definitely winding down. It is a poem about aging—I can see that now, but it has been one of my favorite poems since I first read its wistful lines in high school and they corresponded with my own adolescent sense of longing—longing to . . . embark on my life, to . . . depart, to set forth. Hungry. Restless. I even based a college application essay on this poem. What I love here is how the narrator embraces life:

> I cannot rest from travel; I will drink
> Life to the lees. All times I have enjoyed
> Greatly, have suffered greatly, both with those
> That loved me, and alone.
> I am become a name;
> For always roaming with a hungry heart
> Much have I seen and known—cities of men
> And manners, climates, councils, governments,
> Myself not least, but honored of them all—
> And drunk delight of battle with my peers,
> Far on the ringing plains of windy Troy.
> . . . How dull it is to pause, to make an end,
> To rust unburnished, not to shine in use!

There it is: the desire of each of us to express our full potential, to "shine in use." What brings out our ability, and enables us to be used by society, and valued? Is it not the vision of an educator, who in the leadership role identifies skills, provides strategies and opportunities to develop and express them, and supports that developmental work, all in the name of what our community needs. Thus, in developing ourselves, we each become heroic, noble in our service of society. "You can do this!" Leaders make this encouragement self-serving: "we not only believe in you, we need you!" This, it seems to me, is the message we give as teachers, a message that transforms our students' potential. Our students need this vision of their essential roles in our lives. It is the same message we give in each social and organizational role we play, as coach, parent, colleague, administrator, partner, boss, lover. "You can do this. We need you."

Tennyson is encouraging about what can be accomplished when we work collaboratively and respectfully within our learning community, in a recognition that each other is necessary to achieve our ends:

> . . . Come, my friends,
> Tis not too late to seek a newer world.
> . . . Though much is taken, much abides; and though
> We are not now that strength which in the old days
> Moved earth and heaven, that which we are, we are—
> One equal temper of heroic hearts,
> Made weak by time and fate, but strong in will,
> To strive, to seek, to find, and not to yield.

I see the poem as about not endings, but encouragement for always new beginnings. It seems to me that the vision that enables us to look upon each other with a measure of hope for what someone can contribute is one of love. This vision comes from a sense of responsibility for each other. Love is at the heart of the vision that makes people feel recognized and valued. Love imparts a sense of belonging, and thus, the connection to community becomes itself a means of recognition and value.

But I see forgiveness as well in Tennyson's poem. Think of the word itself, for*give*ness, grounded in the act of giving, something you do on behalf of someone, based on love. The narrator's memory of community and fellowship is so strong that he yearns to recover it. In many ways, he wants to be a student again, setting out to explore the world:

. . . for my purpose holds
To sail beyond the sunset, and the baths
Of all the western stars, until I die

And this gray spirit yearning in desire
To follow knowledge like a sinking star
Beyond the utmost bound of human thought.

He is *three legs in the afternoon,* but rather than be resigned to living with memories, "barren," "aged," or "idle," he wants still to engage in a ceaseless quest. He is forgiving of himself and of his stage in life:

You and I are old;
Old age hath yet his honor and his toil.
Death closes all; but something ere the end,
Some work of noble note, may yet be done,
Not unbecoming men that strove with Gods.

Such a vision is not only generative, it is heroic. Perhaps the ability to recognize in one another the capacity to undertake growth, to take risks, to endure vulnerability, to express ambition, to forge plans, and continuously to make an effort to do better, are each imaginative acts grounded in love and forgiveness of ourselves and of each other. It is a generous vision that transcends limitations and obstacles that people present in the transactions of learning. Perhaps forgiveness is the sibling of hope, a commitment to see the best and the potential in everyone and in every situation. A leader of any community, whether a teacher in a course, or an administrator of a university, or a responsible parent in a family, is challenged spiritually and intellectually, faced with doubts and fears about the capacity of oneself or one's group to grow, to learn, to change.

And in this challenge I see a resource in the world of science, a concept that originally meant "knowledge." The emergent field of whole dynamical systems, sometimes characterized as chaos theory, complexity theory, consilience theory, and other theories that strive to express how the "whole" operates, sheds new light on learning as a process of change. These theories describe how systems defined by change, complexity, interdependence, and the diversity of elements that comprise them, operate in a coherent, orderly manner that is not usually visible or transparent, especially from the viewpoint of someone inside the system.

For example, it is usually not possible or at least intuitive to see the order in turbulence, or turbulence's patterns, as with weather, unless we step back in time and space. We know that energy entering a system causes initial disturbances which then "self-organize" as the system achieves stability or equilibrium. From afar, is possible to see the order that exists within a system, no matter how confused, chaotic, or conflicting it may seem up close. Our earth, from this vantage, can be seen "whole" as simultaneously dark and light, wet and dry, cold and hot. As one coherent system it contains multiple co-existing realities. Our classroom is such a system. Each student is such a system. Energy enters, in the form of a new idea, a question, an assignment, a world view different from one's own. Mental order is challenged. Students can be demoralized in the process. In their confusion, they can doubt themselves and their own capacity to learn. They can doubt their teacher's capacity, or the institution itself, or their program. The teacher here has a great opportunity to help the students "forgive" themselves and the learning environment which has destabilized their knowledge. The teacher can envision "the whole" of the student's potential over time to learn and change and grow. The student is the "human being" who is at once *four legs in the morning, two legs at noon,* and *three legs in the afternoon.* At the very moment when the student is most vulnerable, the teacher's integrated vision is one of possibility and potential and faith.

Teaching is joyous because we engage with humanity in a vision of what someone can be that is grounded in love and optimism. We can enable people to develop and express their whole selves over time, growing stronger and wiser. As I reflect on the opportunities I have had in my life to serve our community, and realize the extent of my debt to others whose leadership has included a recognition of what I could give, I also can see how leadership is rooted not only giving a vision, but forgiving. How many times I have not lived up to the vision of what I could do or be, and what has it taken to keep on, trying to do my best, to do justice to the faith in me that someone has had? How forgiving have the leaders and teachers in my life been, how loving, and how full of faith in what happens when you believe in someone and in the unsteady, unpredictable, turbulent processes we call learning and professional development. "I am a part of all that I have met." The love, leadership, and forgiveness of the teachers in my life have made me grateful and resilient, open to new experience and challenge and risk. And that is what we give back, when our students stumble and fail and resist the changes that learning requires, the changes that make us unrecognizable to ourselves, the changes that make our worldviews seem foreign to us, and our confidence waver in what we know. As learners we need someone to know the stages, to forgive and even love when we fail; and that ability to see each other whole over time must be what the Sphinx was insisting on as a necessary quality in all citizens.

I doubt that we can have joy without a sense of risk, or joy's companion, earnest doubt. Both are forms of a consciousness that does not take for granted what can happen when you open yourself to change and hardly recognize yourself as you become something new, and more complex. I think all teachers would agree with Tennyson's hero the not-yet-weary Ulysses, who says,

All times I have enjoyed greatly, and suffered greatly

We can't have one without the other. Arising at 3 a.m. to worry about that day's class, sure one is not prepared enough, that it will not go well, dealing with students struggling with doubts about their ability to understand and express the material: we all go through this no matter how many courses we have taught or prizes we have won or books we have published. In leadership, forgiveness, and love, we never give up, we never stop caring. We never rest from "travel"—our blessed worries. And our joy, our joy when our students light up with a vision of what they can be and do, and how they are needed: who would ever want another kind of life? I don't think teachers ever become complacent. But we can savor the gratitude of being in this profession which keeps us new, and spiritually, at least, always *four feet in the morning,* despite our gray hairs and frazzled worries.

* * * * *

D r. Barbara Mossberg's commitment to teaching has earned her distinguished teaching awards and recognition from Indiana University (William Riley Parker Prize, University of Oregon) (Ersted Award, Mortar Board) University of Helsinki (Rector's Medal of Honor), Danforth Foundation (associate), Mellon Foundation (fellow, Aspen Institute for Humanistic Studies). She has had several senior Fulbrights, including Senior Fulbright Distinguished Lecturer. Appointed U.S. Scholar in Residence, Dr. Mossberg represented American higher education and culture at the federal level. She has lectured and consulted in more than 30 countries, and has served as a senior fellow at the American Council of

Education. Her leadership includes serving as tenured professor at the University of Oregon, academic administrative roles supporting curricular and faculty development at the University of Oregon, Hobart and William Smith Colleges, National University and at Goddard College as president. Currently, Dr. Moseberg serves as a professor and Director for Integrated Studies at California State University at Monterey Bay and as a Visiting Scholar at the James Macgregor Burns Academy of Leadership. She serves as senior consultant at the American Council on Education, Center for Institutional Initiatives, and Senior Research scholar, National Council for Research on Woman. Several adversary boards for environmental and global education include her as a member. Recently publications include a book of essays on John Muir and commissioned articles for Peter Lang's Higher Education Series, Fulbright Scholar collection and for The Presidency. Her presentations have included the Library of Congress Mandate on Education, Council for International Exchange of Scholars and the American Academy Council on Education.